Rock the Kasbah

ROCK ON!

MARIE

# Rock the Kasbah

## A Memoir of Misadventure

Marie Loerzel

Elemental Press
Lafayette, Colorado

**Rock the Kasbah: A Memoir of Misadventure**



Printed and bound in the United States of America.
Elemental Press. 

ISBN: 978-0-9912036-0-4

Cover art by Lisa Perzentka
Interior design and layout: Juanita Dix

*For Craig, my rock.*

## Acknowledgements

This is the place where I get to express my unending gratitude to all the people who helped me make *Rock the Kasbah*, the book, more than just a figment of my imagination.

Leah Griffith, my mentor, for leading the way and encouraging me to find my own path at the same time.

Laine Cunningham, for urging me to dig deeper to bring the story to life and giving me some authorly-ish skills along the way.

Victoria Young, the most meticulous and supportive proofreader and friend a girl could ask for.

Lisa Perzentka, for your time and talent in taking my cover idea and making it into a work of art.

My faithful blog readers, who welcomed me and my family into your daily lives.

My world-wide network of girlfriends, who have always appreciated me for the dorky nut job I truly am. You have supported me, cheered me on and laughed with me. Often, at me.

My parents for giving me my bi-nationality. So I would never run out of material to write about or ways to make fun of myself. Ever.

My family, for enduring my dinners, photo-ops, urgent need to bump you off the computer at a moments notice to write, using you as fodder and for putting up with me in general. Without you life would be mundane and meaningless. (Not to mention, I'd have much less to write about.)

And you. For taking a chance on me and reading *Rock the Kasbah*.

# Chapter 1

## Invisible Ninja

My therapist fervently searched my face for clues. Distress? Anger? Admission? Anything at all? But I'm no emotion whore. I don't just give it away.

Her question swirled weightlessly overhead as my body stayed cemented to the black pleather chair. Immobility prevented the synthetic material from emitting fart sounds. By remaining quiet and still, I was safe from saying the wrong thing. And from emitting foul body noises. I was almost invisible, a stealth ninja complete with Chinese throwing stars. Except I'm half-Canadian. And everyone knows Canadians aren't mean enough to use weapons. Which was why I definitely didn't own throwing stars. Canadians are polite. Obnoxiously polite. Which must be why I paid this woman $110 an hour to probe me and tick off every slow second while I daydreamed about ninjas.

After two entirely painful minutes of feigned contemplation—which was actually spent distracting myself with more bemused thoughts—I answered "No?" emphatically and quizzically.

She looked directly into my eyes. I was a disobedient dog who couldn't match her gaze. So I scanned the room for anything to dilute the intensity. The tense tendons of her hands exposed her effort at artificial patience. I must have given her the wrong answer. Dammit, I had so tried to get that one right! She said there's no right or wrong in therapy. That's total shrink bullshit. I usually excel at giving people exactly what they want in a very gold-star worthy way.

I'd already wasted more than half the session trying to distract her. Confessed I hadn't realized a big hole in the ass of my jeans exposed my underwear until I'd arrived in the parking lot. When I'd realized that a panty show and tell might have been inappropriate, I'd switched to discussing the magazines in her outer office.

"I think that cover photo on *Us* of ever-perky Drew Barrymore made me even more depressed in the two minutes I was waiting. Have you ever considered a *Mad* magazine subscription? Seriously, how perfect would that be for a psychologist?"

My Conan monolog had stopped short when she hadn't reacted. Nothing. My attempts at comic relief usually at least mildly entertained people so they didn't realize I was disconnecting from meaningful conversation. Maybe she didn't have a sense of humor. Or maybe she was one of those Type A laser-focused people who couldn't tolerate distractions or anything that doesn't produce results. Either way, it sucked.

That's when I silently waited for her to start fixing me. I hoped it wouldn't involve reflecting and talking about my feelings because I hated that shit. So I started calculating. I'm not good at math or anything but I figured I'd paid almost $2 to avoid talking to her while trying to make her happy at the same time. Except, obviously, I was destined to fail to reach at least one of those goals. And more than likely to default on both. It made me so curiously comfortable I tucked one leg under the other and a synthetic fart squeaked out.

"No, I'm not a perfectionist with codependent tendencies," I said with a throaty chuckle.

Definitely not. What was she thinking? I was way too imperfect to be a perfectionist. Plus, I wasn't dependent on anything. Although

I was dependable to a fault. I would do anything for anyone at any time. Especially for people who were toxic waste dumps of needs who wouldn't appreciate it. Then I'd be forced to dumpster dive with reckless abandon even if they implored me not to.

"Marie," my therapist said, "I don't think this is a good time for you to move to Africa."

The intimacy of her using my first name was startling. That sentence had been tailored just for me. Even though it was clear that she completely didn't get me. I'd been there for weeks by that point. Not talking, not crying, not divulging the torrid details of my life, and that was the crap she came up with? For someone who was trained in what's going on in other people's heads, she clearly lacked insight. Although I would never have told her that because I hate confrontation.

"Is there any way you can postpone moving by just a few months?" she asked. "Your marriage is fragile right now. And I don't know if there will be any kind of mental health programs there to support you."

Oh god, did she just use the term *mental health?* Psychotic puppy killers who wear diapers need mental health plans. I just needed someone to completely ignore me, shatter my dreams, and make me feel completely inadequate. And to be honest, my husband was really shitty at that. He was all supportive, interested and attentive. Which might be why I felt after all this time that maybe we just weren't right for each other. He was a complete and independent person who didn't need me to fix him. I felt like my natural talents might be wasted. I could put them to better use by rescuing a douchebag. It would be my gift to the world. You know, denying my own needs. Which was pretty easy because I didn't even know what my needs were. And I had no idea how to figure them out.

I've always been the girl with potential. Who could really go places and achieve things. Everyone around me always believed that… except me. I'd insulated myself with a healthy layer of self-doubt and deprecation. It was the only thing I was truly awesome at. After all those years, I was nearly perfect at cutting myself down. So why the hell would I want to give that up by delving deep into my psyche now?

Because my husband had insisted I go to therapy. Since I'd always given people what they wanted, I did it for him. I never would have come on my own. I'd much rather be at a thrift store searching for a pair of funky, clunky orange heels I would never wear because they'd be much too uncomfortable. So what if I spent some days in bed crying? Or if most days it was way too much effort to cry without a dealer who made house calls to deliver artificial tears? You know, the really pure stuff. Because I was empty. So empty I didn't even need food any more. Nothing could fill me up. All I wanted to do was sleep.

Of course, I'd never tell anyone that. Because the only thing more painful than having needs was expressing those needs so someone could help me. And I didn't need help. That would only inhibit my visceral compulsion to help others who were beyond my help.

"It's all set," I said. "We're leaving in a few weeks. We'll be fine."

I flashed the closed-mouth smirk I reserved for smoothing things over. The truth was, I didn't know if we would be fine. And I really didn't care. I just wanted to escape. To break up with her and for her to forget all about me. Which was what I always assumed people did. Although I wanted to do it gently so she'd feel like an incredible therapist who'd cured me of all my ills. I'd live happily ever after and all that Cinderella shit.

Fairy tales bear no resemblance to real life. Once Cinderella married Prince Charming and had four kids who innocently sucked up every minute of her time and every ounce of her energy, she didn't have anything left for her prince. In fact, she'd never spent much time with him before the kids had come along. Cinderella had been too damn busy getting a master's degree and establishing a career. And Prince Charming had been in medical school and smelled like formaldehyde for four entire years and only came home to eat, study or sleep. After that came three years of residency so he smelled like B.O. after working twenty-four hour shifts. Then when the kids came along, Cinderella and Prince Charming were too busy merely existing to spare time for each other. Though they wound up sleeping in the same bed at night, they were alone. Together.

~

I tried to reserve what little energy I had for my kids. Which meant neglecting my husband Craig. He wasn't home enough for me to consider his needs anyhow because he worked long hours as the pediatrician loved by patients and their mothers. Especially young moms who wore their best cleavage-baring blouses to their kids' check-ups, and that wasn't to make breast feeding more convenient. They wanted to impress the young doctor with the piercing blue eyes, light brown hair and Billy Baldwin-esque good looks. Leading me to believe that if I died, there would be a long line of single moms comforting my husband in their bosoms. Which I'm not endowed with.

Squinting at me from across a dimly lit room one might think, I bore a non-striking resemblance to Jennifer Love Hewitt. Except I was taller with stringy curly hair, was less hippy, and was at least a full bra cup size smaller. Basically I looked like the skinny girl who sat behind you in high school math class that never talked to anyone. Moving to Senegal meant no one would confuse us for our celebrity doppelgangers for a full two and half years. Over there, no one would know who those celebrities were. Plus, I was positive I would blend seamlessly into a brunette-dominated culture where women meticulously covered their assets.

We would be completely anonymous with no past trailing behind us and no obligations. No family, no friends, and absolutely nothing to do. It would be a break from the stress of our normal lives. That was the delusion, anyhow. Craig would work for the Peace Corps, we still had four kids, I still had my insecurities, and as it turned out, nothing about Africa came stress-free.

We'd already told the kids we were moving to Senegal. They took the news well. In their minds, it was an extended vacation with pony rides, eating macaroni and cheese and soda at a restaurant every night, and all the unbridled happiness that came with it. That was our fault. We marketed it as a fun adventure. We were even naive enough to believe the fantasy ourselves. That we could simply outrun our problems by crossing a tumultuous ocean without capsizing.

We were headed across the Atlantic with our own worst enemies...us. Three out of the four kids couldn't stand each other. Craig and I, while functional on a peripheral level, weren't connected. We needed life preservers to keep us afloat while we frantically dogpaddled and tried to pull the kids to shore. Without knowing if we'd end up ravaged on the same deserted island. Without a support system of family and friends.

Not only that, since my youngest was old enough to start kindergarten, all the kids would be in school in a few months. For years I'd dreaded the transition. I would be a stay-at-home mom without any kids at home. American culture dictated that I should either get a job or homeschool. I didn't want to take a job I hated for the sake of working. I wanted a job that fit me, that I loved. Besides, continuing to love my kids dictated that I shouldn't homeschool them.

What kind of mother did that make me? Did I still have value as a woman? That question was especially important. We were moving to Africa, a continent where being a woman equated to being a second-class citizen. I couldn't have known then that I'd claim my voice and my freedom in Morocco.

~

The blog started as a simple solution to keep in touch with friends and family. We didn't know if phone service would be consistent or just consistently expensive. How else would anyone know that we hadn't died in a massive lamb-herding accident? So we turned to the worldwide web. It was everywhere. It had *world* in the name, right? That's how the blog started. I couldn't talk to everyone individually and tell the same story over and over again. But I could write and post pictures in a very impersonal blog post available for mass consumption. Convenient, unobtrusive, and most important, free. In January of 2010, Rock The Kasbah was born.

At first the name didn't make sense. Senegal is in sub-Saharan Africa and there aren't any kasbahs there. Kasbahs are ancient walled cities native to northern Africa, not West Africa. Since I'm stubborn, the fact that it didn't make sense didn't stop me. I would make it fit. Besides, The Clash's song *Rock the Casbah* was one of my all-time favorites. Some people said the song was about Africa's anti-imperialist sentiment, which had largely been French's bitch back in the day. Most neurotic hipster audiophiles agree that the song was actually written about the ban Algerian Islamist authorities had on popular music from the West from the 70's through the 90's. Even though the ban was instituted in 1979 by the Ayatollah Khomeini in Iran. If you confer with the Urban Dictionary, the term "*rock the casbah*" means disobeying authority and doing something you believe is right even though it isn't legal. This proved prophetic later on.

Then again, it's also slang for sex.

Pick your favorite and let's just say that's why I named it that.

What follows is one of my first blog posts. About hoarding real things, not just my emotions.

## HOARDING

Reality has set in. We're moving to Africa. We're really going. Which means there's really a lot to do. Big important stuff like renting out the house, so we have to get the house ready to rent out. Sell the cars, enroll the kids in school, taxes, financial stuff, storage, learning French, and the dental appointment I've been putting off for two years. Don't forget that mammogram I was supposed to get when I turned forty a couple months ago. That's not on the agenda today, though.

Panic is setting in. We need to load up on stuff we won't be able to get there. I have no idea what we can get there. Thus the conundrum. I start ticking off a list of essentials we just can't live without. Chapstick. I'm addicted to lip balm and freely admit I'm powerless and can't wean myself from its waxy sheen. What about hair conditioner for the girls? Surely they won't sell it in a cute convenient spray bottle sporting a purple octopus. Unless it's actually green. Perhaps most important—the palest white people in America let alone Africa need sunscreen. Lots of sunscreen!

Panic + avoidance of urgent matters = emergency trip to Target. Where do I even start? The kids will need shorts, sandals and t-shirts but they're in school. If I choose the shorts the kids won't wear them. That would require another trip with the unwilling kids to return the shorts accompanied by melodic whining, incessant complaining, and mandatory poking. Anyway, it's winter and there aren't any sandals in all of Colorado Springs. I've already massively reduced my scope by excluding the kids.

Everyone else in the family has a good bike except for me. Mine cost fifteen dollars at a thrift store. When I got it home, the brakes didn't work. I imagine exploring Dakar, the capital of Senegal, and its markets on my bike. It's got a vintage bell and the basket attached to the handlebars is chock full of fresh organic local fruits and veggies. I'm wearing a strappy sundress with a floppy hat and sunglasses, and I'm doused in sunscreen with silken shaved legs. This is a fantasy because I don't wear sundresses or anything that needs ironing. And I have 5 o'clock shadow on my legs by 10 a.m. I blame my Hungarian heritage. I don't know anything about driving there, so biking might be my only source of transportation. Oh my god, I need a bike this instant! Wait a minute. I don't know anything about bikes, which is why I bought one without brakes. Ok, I should probably research online first. Who am I kidding? Craig will research it.

Hmmm. What's bike riding without music? I should totally get an MP3 player. Does Craig have one? Maybe we can just share it. There's always CDs. I could get a new one and download it onto our shared MP3 player. The Best of the Clash perhaps? Doesn't buying a CD defeat the purpose if I am just going to download it? I don't even know if we have a converter for Senegalese voltage. Dammit, I suck at hoarding.

So, I move on to toiletries. What kind of sunscreen was it that didn't make my face break out? Oh man, I'll have to go home and check the label.

You get the picture.

Here's the final tally of purchases:

- One small tube of Neutrogena Sport SPF 70 sunscreen for the face. I think this is the stuff that doesn't make me break out. I'll test it before I commit to a larger quantity. In the interim, they might create an SPF 100 version. I'm definitely gonna need that!
- Four tubes of organic orange ginger lip balm. On sale for $2.50 per tube. I would have bought more but four was all they had left.
- Four tubes of St. Ives apricot facial scrub. On sale for $2.89 per tube. This is a no-brainer. It's on sale and if I don't want to use it on my face I can always scour the pots or bathtub with it.
- Ten bottles of Suave kid's hair detangler. Without it, Jade and Ember bear an uncanny resemblance to the kids in the desert from Mad Max Beyond Thunderdome. I'm betting that Senegal does not have Suave hair detangler. It's a gut feeling that they'd probably use something like liquefied pig lard instead.
- Two packs of razors I randomly threw in the cart. My only qualification was that they not be pink, purple or mint green, colors I despise. Not that the color matters. Or even that I have one. In Africa, I might be the only one with bald pits and legs.

When I got to the checkout and loaded my pathetic purchases on the belt, I realized I'd forgotten to pick up a birthday gift for one of the kid's friends. The party is tomorrow. Everyone knows that once you've got stuff on the belt, it's too late. It's already yours even though you haven't paid for it. And hell if I'm going all the way back to toys. I didn't even think about toys and what my kids would get other kids for their birthdays in Africa.

Three bags. I hardly bought anything! What happened to hoarding? I have some hoarding in my genes; I should be awesome. But I'm pathetic!

Tomorrow I'm going to schedule that dental appointment. No. Wait. I'll call about the mammogram. Because I'd rather have my boobs squished than my teeth drilled. Unless I should finish painting the living room, fill out the applications to enroll the kids, or start learning French.

# *Chapter 2*

# Yellow Fever, Typhoid and Malaria, Oh My

It was my idea to name our kids after the elements. I'm the non-practical, transcendentalist half of our marriage. At the time, I thought it was all poetic and symbolic of them being the elements of our universe. These of course are some of the beautiful ideations you have before you're a parent and realize kids are elementally the biggest source of frustration, agony and stress in a marriage. I mean that in the most lovingly realistic way.

As our kids grew, we saw that each was like the element they were named after. Our oldest, Sky, at eleven is our air child. For clarification, he's a boy. This causes a lot of confusion when making airline reservations, medical appointments, or anything that requires paperwork without visual validation that he is in fact male. He's very masculine with his coarse, curly brown hair and strong brow. His beautiful green eyes are embellished with long perfectly curled lashes that are the envy of every girl everywhere. He's extremely idealistic yet lacks the practicality required for everyday living. Like picking a wet towel off the floor. He takes everything apart and dissects it to see how it works.

He also falsely believes he's in charge of everyone else, and everyone in the house knows it. They manipulate him by playing into his deep desire to be an authority figure when they need their MP3 players fixed. He's like the wind. He's either completely unfocused or blowing concentrated hot air directly in your face.

River, our water boy and Sky's Irish twin, is a mere eleven months younger. They're not biologically related because all our kids are adopted and none are an ounce Irish. With his straight blond hair, blue eyes and delicate features, he looks like the impossible lovechild of Macaulay Culkin and Kurt Cobain. He's the complete opposite of his brother and content to let Sky do all the work and bail him out as needed. Basically constantly. He's a typical second child even though we adopted him first. He's a stickler for rules and thoughtfully reminds everyone about them through frequent public service announcements. He has boundless energy and doesn't stop moving, just like a river, though he acts like a quirky old man. Which is why he is Old Man Lazy River.

Jade, our oldest daughter, is eight but far beyond her years in maturity. Her long, dirty blond hair is sun-kissed and her big eyes turned from blue to a namesake green soon after we brought her home. She's the happy hippy who loves everyone and every creature. She even sunscreens potato bugs. She's completely grounded and has quietly appointed herself family peace keeper when disputes arise. Which is all the time. She's the only calming presence in the house, including me. She's our nurturing mother earth. I foresee many future Thanksgivings organized, cooked and hosted by her because that definitely won't be at her sister's house.

The last element, of course, is fire. At four years old Ember is the true mastermind. She runs the entire house. She may look all-American with her strawberry blonde hair, green eyes and freckled apple-pie face. But she's a Russian spy. As the youngest, she's highly competitive and knows how to plot and manipulate to get what she thinks she deserves. Technically she would be called the baby but she's never been a baby. She'd eat that baby for breakfast. And she's a pyromaniac. We wouldn't know that until later, though.

Don't worry, even though none of the elements are biological siblings, they hate each other as much as if they were. The ultimate rivalry is between archenemies River and Ember. Fire and water do not mix after all.

I did this to myself. Craig, the logical, rational side of our marriage and the voice of reason, really dropped the ball by letting this whole naming thing happen. We should have gone with Judicious, Idle, Emphatic and Serenity. Although how boring would that be?

We were moving to Africa for them. So they could see what's truly important in life and appreciate it. Entitlement, crap TV and the crap sold on TV was what's wrong with this generation. Oh, and Chuck E. Cheese. They needed to see the starving children in Africa doing without so they could understand that small things aren't small at all when you don't have them. Like food. It was easy to take corn-fed chicken, modified corn starch, mono-, tri- and di-glycerides, dextrose, lecithin, chicken broth, yellow corn flour, vegetable shortening, partially hydrogenated corn oil and citric acid fried up fresh every twenty-five minutes for granted.

I wanted them to be exposed to real food all the time and to see it as fuel and sustenance. Not as hurried, wasteful, empty entertainment. I wanted to be able to walk outside my door and give the dinner they whined about to a hungry child who would scarf it down even if they hated it. Most of all, Craig and I wanted the elements to experience the world's diversity. That just wasn't possible from an armchair in homogenous Colorado Springs even if we subscribed to the Travel and National Geographic channels (which we're too cheap to do).

Before we did any of this crucial teaching of life lessons by denying the elements their comforts, I bribed them with candy bars. After all, it was the great American way and we weren't in Morocco yet. So we didn't have to start being good role models until later.

The day lives in infamy as *Happy, Fun Candy Day*. It didn't start out happy or fun. Just mandatory. Going to Africa meant getting shots for all the scary diseases we could be exposed to there. So I stopped the car at Walgreens and said, "Pick out anything you want. King size it, why don't you?" Which marked the first and hopefully the last time I said that, although I can't make any promises.

It wasn't for the elements' benefit so much as mine. I didn't like pain and since I had to get four shots too and I'd heard that yellow fever hurt like a karate kick to the knee, I wanted something to look forward to. So, damn straight I was gonna chase it down with a gargantuan Snickers bar and a sugar high. Turned out the shots weren't that bad but I still sucked down that king size Snickers in record time.

Everything was set. The house was up for rent. The kids were registered at their new school. Our essentials were sorted, packed and shipped. We had our passports, visas and airplane tickets. Craig took a sabbatical from his pediatric practice. His new job as regional medical officer of West Africa meant a huge pay cut, trading out babies for adult Peace Corps volunteers, and lots of travel to check on Peace Corps clinics. He'd treated adults when he'd been in the Army and deployed to Iraq. Apparently being a pediatrician hadn't prevented him from being deployed to treat adults. The Army's take was that we were all just big kids anyway. Which might explain some of the war games.

It sounded like he'd be away from the family a lot during our trip but we were used to that already. So the plan didn't seem all that much different except that by being a doctor in Africa, he'd get to see all kinds of diseases he'd never see in America. Pathologically speaking, that's just the kind of thing that really excited him.

Since I wasn't working, the only thing I had to give up was roller derby. I'd been skating on a league for two years. Joining the team was the first thing I'd done for myself since becoming a mother. Sure, I sucked and spent far more time face-down learning to identify floor cleaners by scent and sheen than intimidating or knocking down anyone else. I still loved every minute. It was my chance to get out of the house and to be something other than just my kids' mom. I loved being surrounded by women. Most were younger than me but while I was skating, none of the details mattered. Not age, occupation, ethnicity, tattoo count, sexual orientation or body size. All that mattered was you had something to prove and a really cool alter ego derby name with which to do it.

Mine was Bad Mojo. She was foulmouthed and tougher than me. She'd take a hit directly into a cement wall and get right back up and do it all over again. And she could stay up past 11 p.m. because practices were late at night after the rink closed. I was reluctant to resign from the league because I loved getting beat to a pulp so much. I also worried that I would retire the mojo I'd worked so hard to accrue.

~

A few days before our departure, we were living out of suitcases at the Embassy Suites. Craig and I enjoyed the free happy hour every night while the elements made it to school every morning despite Shirley Temple hangovers.

Then the Peace Corps called. Plans had changed. We weren't moving to Senegal. Instead we were headed to Morocco. All I knew about Morocco was that Hotel Farah had been bombed in 2003 and the U.S. government had issued a travel warning for Americans. It had foiled our travel plans at the time. We'd salvaged the trip by diverting to Tunisia, the most peaceful country in the region at the time.

Seven years later, not only were we going on the trip of a lifetime but we got to live there. Even though our possessions were headed for Senegal. Maybe we'd meet up again one day. Maybe not. It didn't even matter. We didn't need stuff. We'd probably be living in a mud hut anyway.

~

That March Morocco welcomed us with lush greenery provided courtesy of the endless, depressing, Seattle-esque rain. The rainy winter season was near its end and Rabat, the country's capital, was our new home. The scent of jasmine and orange blossoms filled the air. Unless you were in the oldest part of the city in the medina where a symphony of fish, cumin, olives mixed with B.O. and trash reigned. Most foreign dignitaries in Morocco were stationed among the embassies, nonprofits, and the Peace Corps' provincial office.

The city was big enough to have a McDonald's and a sacrilegious TGIFriday's that didn't serve alcohol, but not cosmopolitan enough to have a Starbucks or a Gap. We were disappointed that they had any American companies, especially fast food, because we were there to cut ties with consumerism. Not to worry. McDonalds wasn't at all like the ones in the states. Morocco's had McFondue burgers. I know because it was plastered on billboards all over the city.

Even though Rabat was the second largest city in Morocco after Casablanca (which did have a Starbucks and a Gap), it had a small town feel. Most roads didn't have street signs. Which meant we got around by getting lost in a maze where every building was painted white until we eventually noticed one of those houses had a slightly green door and eventually that we needed to turn left there to get out. To do that, we dodged donkey carts, mopeds, cows and cars. It would have been far easier to train for the Olympic steeplechase. Then we wouldn't have to learn Arabic or worry about getting attacked by one of the feral cats that roamed the potholed, garbage-strewn streets.

Neighborhoods within the city were a complete mystery. Everything was shrouded behind white gates that surrounded white houses. Some said they provided security while others claimed the gates preserved a sense of modesty for the fraction of flashy, huge-ass mansions scattered about town. Since there was a huge discrepancy between the rich and poor with no middle class to speak of, having a huge house chock full of stuff meant that inevitably someone was gonna want to steal your stuff.

Although we expected no-frills housing, we ended up sandwiched between the ambassador of Oman and the general of the Moroccan army. The museum-sized house boasted twelve-foot ceilings, a grand entryway, marble floors and five bathrooms but only three bedrooms. Oh, and it came with a man-maid named Mohammed. The complete opposite of a mud hut. This wasn't a house for relaxed family living; it was a formal house built to entertain and impress people.

We weren't impressed. I didn't need a maid but societal norms dictated that I did. Luckily, I scored the only man-maid in the whole city. Mohammed became our symbol of gender equality in a very male-dominated culture. What he lacked in physical stature he more than made up for with hard work. An honest family man with five children who matched the ages of our own. He washed our dishes, cleaned our showers, and mopped two football fields of tile three times a week. The other two days he spent in the garden, his favorite place, with his apprentice Jade.

The kids started school the day after we arrived. They were all groggy and disoriented from jet lag except Ember. She was the only kid dying to go to school but she wouldn't start kindergarten until the following academic year, five long months away. She got the double bonus of having to stay home with me and being dragged around Morocco as I figured out how the hell to get things done without knowing the language. She was my constant companion as I hailed taxis for trips to the grocery store, searched for working ATMs, tried to speak French, and wondered what in the world Moroccans had against street signs.

She despised every minute. I tried to mix in fun things like trips to the park but with her exotic Caucasian-ness and English language, Moroccan kids gathered around to paw her pin-straight, flaxen hair. By far the worst for her was when strangers approached and kissed her on top of the head if she were lucky. They delivered the kiss to the cheek or mouth if they thought she was a talisman. She quickly came to hate being a cute blond girl in Morocco. I stopped taking her to the playground to have mandatory fun that ended in her being molested.

This was nothing like I'd expected. In a way, I was disappointed that we weren't forced to live in squalor and wouldn't need to drink our own urine when the village well dried up. I hadn't expected to live like pseudo-royalty among ambassadors, generals, and counselors to the King. It had never occurred to me that the elements would attend school with the children of influential people. But that's exactly what happened.

That's also why my kids have a completely twisted view of Moroccan kids. They went to school with the .005% of the population that was completely loaded. A fact that didn't escape them. The wealth was even worse than the consumerism we thought we'd left back in America. The elements liked the school's laid-back structure and the long lunches spent at picnic tables, but that was about it.

The first week of school, a girl named Allah (the Arabic word for god) told Sky she could get anything she wanted for lunch. To prove her point, the next day her driver appeared promptly to hand-deliver a personal pan Pizza Hut pie to Sky. The act solidified her social standing and the fact that she was related to the King and proved she was a total freaking spoiled brat. We'd entered a microcosm in the mecca of materialism.

A disappointment nearly as big was the produce. Fruits and vegetables grown in developing countries isn't all organic. Guess who buys the pesticides that are banned from use in America? Yup. Most of Africa.

On top of all that, Craig started work with the Peace Corps right away. In Colorado he brought home boring stories of kids with the flu. Every once in a while something exciting would happen...a kid would stick a Band-Aid up his nose and Craig would have to extract it. But his work was fairly routine and, to me as I listened to the mundane details of his day, a bit boring. That completely changed as he began treating adults. Or really big kids who pretended to be adults because they needed a twenty-minute phone tutorial to be walked through taking a Benadryl for their colds.

Most Peace Corps volunteers were recent college grads in their twenties. Often they were taking their first trip abroad without having their parents on speed-dial whenever they needed to ask how much laundry detergent to use. They lived in remote villages all alone teaching English or business skills or starting up health programs. Sometimes they worked without an internet connection, so they didn't even have Facebook.

Craig saw Moroccan volunteers who needed medical attention. He also coordinated medical care throughout West Africa for volunteers whose needs exceeded local capabilities by flying them to Rabat. Dental hygiene wasn't a priority throughout Africa, so it wasn't uncommon for volunteers to undertake a grueling three-day trek that involved a camel to the clinic with the end result being a root canal. Which sounded horrific unless you'd been living in a remote village in the mountains with cold well water for bathing, eating bread and olives, and drinking mint tea in the same outfit you'd worn all week even after it had been peed on by a pack of mangy cats that stalked your every move because you smelled like the tuna juice that accidentally squirted into your hair three days before. Then the trek and the root canal were positively the best thing that happened to you in the last two years.

Unless you'd contracted an STD from that sketchy volunteer in the next town over who you definitely wouldn't have slept with if they hadn't been the only other person in a sixty-mile radius who could commiserate about how all you really wanted was a box of Kraft macaroni and cheese and some hot water. These were exciting stories. I wanted to hear them all told slowly over a glass of wine as we sat on the porch overlooking the manicured garden sculpted by Mohammed. It was better than watching the Amazing Race on TV, which we didn't have.

While I didn't need television, I was dead set on having something of my own. The disenchantment with our new life sent me in search of a challenge that would distract me from our new reality while wallowing in my inadequacy. I needed to fill the gaping hole that used to be filled with tattooed, tough, catty women who drank too much and talked behind each other's backs. I missed the camaraderie of misfits that was roller derby. I needed to replace it with something.

~

On one of the first days in the country, we were invited to a party of American expats. It didn't take long for the elements to warm up to the other American kids who were also the equivalent of white trash at their exclusive private school. I couldn't waste a second of friend-making time in expat life. My new best friend could be at the party. Even if I had to act like a completely different person who didn't have social anxiety and who's marriage wasn't teetering on the precipice.

That's where I met my new BFF of the month, Agnes (pronounced all Frenchie: On-yes). A funky, outspoken French woman married to an American man. The Chuck Taylors on her feet, standard issue for off-duty derby girls, generated an instant connection. She must have felt it too because she offered to take me to her belly dance class along with my mini-shadow Ember. Bingo. Maybe that could be my something. Even though I broke into a sweat just thinking about walking my dance virgin ass into an intermediate class full of Moroccan women. I swallowed my pride, choked back a gargantuan hunk of fear, and accepted the invitation.

## ASS OLYMPIQUE

There are a few things you should know about me. I'm uncoordinated, I have no belly or hips to speak of, and I'd never taken a dance class of any kind ever before. I'd barely passed aerobics in high school PE. In fact, I still have recurring nightmares about not graduating high school because I fail gym.

I was never much of a girly-girl. In my youth I dug in the dirt, rode my brother's skateboards and flew airplanes. Not only did I act more like a boy, I had a super-short haircut all the way through school. It didn't help that I had no curves to confirm my girlhood. I was a tom boy missing that genetic component other girls seemed to have that made them want to do fun, frivolous things like dance. So why at forty, with some kind of weird genetic mutation and two left feet, would I start now?

We pulled up to the gym where a sign above the door proclaimed ASS Olympique. I assumed that ass had a meaning other than turd originator. The day was hot, so the door was already propped open. A privacy curtain prevented men passing by on the street from looking in. The class was for women's eyes only. A place where they traded their headscarves for hip scarves. In the dressing room, modest *djellabas* were replaced with sparkly, tight, midriff-bearing belly dance costumes. In my tank top and stretchy Old Navy jersey knit skirt, I looked like I was shopping for hummus and Tom's toothpaste at Whole Foods. Substantially overdressed.

Zeinab, the instructor, was Egyptian. She'd married a Moroccan diplomat twenty-five years before and had lived in Morocco ever since. For her act of treachery, her family disowned her. At our first meeting, her name sounded so extraordinary and exotic. Later I learned it's the Arab equivalent to Jennifer. The class was taught in French with some Darija (Moroccan Arabic) thrown in when the conversation grew casual, which happened with some frequency. I didn't speak either language, so I resorted to forced smiling. Unfortunately, I'm pretty sure it conveyed the exact forced aloofness I was trying to conceal.

Right foot where? How did she move her hips like that? Wait. What the hell are my arms supposed to be doing? Shit. My smile disappeared and was replaced with commentary on my every screw up peppered with swear words. No one knew English so it didn't matter how loud I cussed in public. Until I remembered that the first thing you always learn in a foreign language is swear words. Shit. Who cared? No one knew me there. Maybe Ass Olympique needed a mascot. I was gifted at being an ass.

I stumbled through the rest of the class and buried myself discreetly at the back of the room. Which didn't work with the room wallpapered in mirrors. Dammit. My captive belly dance audience, Ember, was judging me. I could feel it. Oh, I know she looked like she was collecting the coins the other dancers shimmied right off their hip scarves. But, I was positive she was embarrassed that her mom was an uncoordinated ass. At the end of class, her worst fear was realized when the dancers kissed her. On the mouth. In America that would have had another context entirely. Child protective services would have been called but that doesn't exist here. Neither does molestation nor the concept of personal space.

I had already decided I was coming back because I love a challenge. And to feel like crap about myself because I never felt like I measured up. Plus, I needed to get out of the house on Tuesdays and Thursdays with a group of older Moroccan women whose languages I don't speak at the expense of my daughter's boundary issues.

# Chapter 3

## Social Disgraces

The elements quickly acclimated to the local culture thanks to the diminutive United Nations of children who rode their bus to and from school. Almost instantaneously they were swear-lingual in both French and Darija. I've always tried to teach them to give back, so they reciprocated the cultural exchange by filling in any holes the locals had in their repertoire of English curses. Not that there were any because the kids at their school saw plenty of transient American kids. I'm positive the elements even learned new swears *en anglais* from that little bastard Spanish kid I always heard stories about. Unless they came from that chubby douchebag Moroccan kid with the glasses who always smiled and said hello in the most subversive Eddie Haskell-ish way. I couldn't stand that kid.

At least the elements hadn't learned any of that crap-talk shit from me. Even though in Morocco, I felt completely liberated to drop the f-bomb out loud in public anywhere I went anytime I was frustrated or defeated. At the supermarket, in traffic, at the ATM, and most definitely at belly dance class. So, all the time, everywhere.

Resorting to expletives disguised my embarrassment over having to communicate with charades because I didn't know French. It's a stupide language. No matter what's said, in French it sounds snobby and condescending. Plus I'm totally crappy at languages.

Not half as crappy as Moroccans were at charades, though. Clearly thumbs-up meant *it's all good.* But the Moroccan interpretation was *fuck you.* Unless it meant *go fuck yourself.* I'm not sure which one exactly. I just wanted to know enough French and Darija to bust my kids when they swore. It was time for French lessons 'cause I was way too lazy to tackle Moroccan Arabic.

Normally I was the one with the ideas but this was Craig's. He had a vested interest in learning the language because doctors and hospitals in Morocco and most of West Africa used French as their official arrogant doctor dialect. For him, it was a professional necessity. I went purely out of duress. I wanted to be fluent in French, I just didn't want to learn it. I'd rather just add *le* to the beginning of every word and use a French accent because I'm apathetic and I don't like homework.

We only attended a few lessons before the instructor had a family emergency that required she move back to Canada. A shortage of maple syrup tappers or something. Since the instructor was leaving, I quit and felt validated not looking for a new one. Since I could count to ten, I considered myself having graduated. Or flunked out. Either way, I decided to spend my time teaching Moroccans the fine art of pantomime without using my thumbs.

Escaping the confines of French class and homework allowed me to conserve energy for pretending I wasn't depressed and didn't have social anxiety. The whole charade of normalcy in a foreign culture where I was constantly forced to meet new people, sometimes in different languages, was exhausting. As an introvert, I was already predisposed to enduring only small spurts of social interaction before I needed to hibernate and listen to The Doors in a dark room.

Since no one wanted to be friends with Debbie Downer, I tried my best to keep up appearances socially. At parties, I lingered at the congested buffet table pretending to eat even though I was still painstakingly disinterested in food and able to eat only negligible portions. Which was completely unlike me. I absolutely, unequivocally loved food. I loved to cook it. I loved to eat it fast and messy. And I loved to share it. Even with introverted anxiety, I could carry off a five-minute conversation about Brussels sprouts. Maybe even a monologue but I'd need to go home immediately after that for introspective time alone to fixate on whether the person I'd talked to had been looking for someone to rescue them from my droning chatter.

In the previous six months I'd gone from stretching the seams of my size 2 pants to wearing a baggy size 0 that needed to be cinched with a belt. I'd wasted away to a 00, and only prepubescent Asian girls should ever be that size. My bladder must have shrunk too because I needed to pee constantly. All the urgent to-and-fro-ing to the bathroom might start rumors I was bulimic. Except I wasn't eating, which technically would have made me anorexic. Since no one knew me, they didn't know I was usually two sizes bigger. And since most females are even more misogynistic than men over body image, I got loads of compliments on my skeletal physique.

The only thing that held my interest less than eating was talking. In any language about anything personal to anyone. I lived in a private world of my own thoughts, insecurities, depression and anxiety. If I kept them to myself, no one would know how truly screwed up and starved I was inside. Plus I didn't want to be a burden and consume someone's time with my petty problems.

So I stopped having meaningful conversations. I found excuses not to call my friends back home. There were some really great ones to choose from. Bad connections, difficult time changes, getting cut off at least once a call and not being able to reconnect. The only time I felt comfortable was when I was uncomfortably alone with an empty stomach and a whirlpool of self-defeating thoughts swirling through my head. Mostly that I wasn't worthy of anyone caring about me.

"I know you don't want to hear this," Craig said one day, "but I've found a couples counselor here who speaks English. She's not trained in couples therapy but she's a psychologist and she's British."

I instantly hated her. And I despised Craig for having researched it behind my back and persuading her to see us. He betrayed all the flagellation I was dishing out. Why the hell wasn't he leaving me alone so I could drown in my misery?

"Her kids go to school with our kids," he said. "Not in the same grades, though."

Holy fuck! Of course they did. The circle of expats was excruciatingly small. Which meant I must have met her or at least seen her before. I flipped through my mental Filofax of all the British people I'd ever seen in Morocco.

In the middle of our conversation, I was overcome with a hypnotic drowsiness. I couldn't keep my eyes open. Against my will, I started to fall asleep. It happened every time Craig started talking about anything intimate we need to fix, anything remotely adverse. Which was an extensive list. I just shut down via emotional narcolepsy.

Our minivan pulled up in front of her gate. Emma counseled people from her children's play room, which consequently didn't make it anymore fun. Her house was on the same street as an American I'd met the week before at a baby shower. With its meticulous, unencumbered perfection, the hostess's American Embassy rental pool housing special looked like a Pottery Barn showroom. She'd worn an off-white silk J. Crew shirt. Her four kids' toys had been tucked away neatly in Ikea bins. Maybe that's where her kids had also been stored because no one could maintain that level of perfection without some malice. What mother wore an expensive off-white wrinkle-free silk

J. Crew blouse without stains on it? Especially with four kids under the age of six? Then again she was Mormon so she didn't have to contend with things that stain like coffee, tea or red wine. Pretty much all that was left was spaghetti sauce and grass stains. Maybe her secret was not playing tackle football while eating spaghetti. I should stop doing that.

Our cover could have been blown any minute by parking our easily identifiable, dented, unwashed Battlecar Galactica in front of the therapist's house. Mrs. Stainfree could drive by in her perfectly clean, cracker-crumb-free minivan at any moment and instantly the word would spread through the expat community…*the Loerzels are in need of mental health.* I could hear the rumors already: "I heard they're puppy killers who wear diapers." We would be shunned from the superficial social lives of the only people who spoke English and therefore the only ones who got that the phrase "That's OK" was a colloquialism that really meant, "No thank you, dumbass." I was too lethargic to start all over and have to explain that to non-native English speakers. Likewise, I didn't want to have British friends obligated to explain that to them, fanny meant vaginal lips. Seriously, it was just too taxing.

Not only were we placed under the microscope by other Americans, as foreigners, someone was always watching. Not just for entertainment purposes, either. Although I liked to believe I possessed some comic genius between tripping over my feet at dance and attempting to roller skate the filthy, potholed, mangy-stray-cat infested streets of Rabat. What had I been thinking to skate on the lawless, pedestrian-unfriendly streets without kneepads or a helmet? I was certain there was a file in someone's office labeled *Blundering Bulimic Girl* with a picture of me picking my nose. On roller skates. Rumor had it that being an informant paid well there and occurred with more frequency than we expats thought.

Emma. How could I hate someone with a name so wholesome and nurturing? It was so *Little House on the Prairie*, the episode where

Caroline was pregnant with her oops child that never made it to air. Yet I did. I hated her. At least I was convinced of that before I met her. She greeted us at the door with her warm, compassionate, I-know-you're-fucked-up-but-I-can-help smile. That's not what won me over, though. The warm, bulky socks that didn't match her outfit did. She probably had to wear a whole size bigger shoe just to accommodate their unseasonable girth. I sympathized with the plight of another diehard sock lover trying to find such enviable ones in a virtual sock-free land. She must have brought them with her from England. Then I smelled the simmering bergamot oil. We might have been wooly sock bergamot soul sisters in another life.

Even so, I would much rather have been stuck in my old French class reciting Voltaire. Anywhere but there. Because I sat in a room with two other people who wanted me to talk about my feelings. Even though I was pretty damn sure I didn't have any. Just when I thought it couldn't get worse, it did. 'Cause just like French class, there was homework. Our homework was to be affectionate. For most people that would be easy, natural even. But it's never been either for me. I could never read the cues for physical contact correctly and I over thought everything, which caused me to have terrible timing. Even with my own family.

Even when the kids were small, I hadn't been a physically demonstrative mom. Greeting them in the morning or at preschool weren't occasions for kissing or hugging unless they initiated it. The two elements we adopted youngest did. River loved to cuddled and would cozy himself in my arms or on my lap. Jade had separation anxiety and clung to me every morning from the start of preschool until the end of first grade.

We adopted Sky and Ember when they'd been older. Both had been stiff and uncomfortable with affection. I'd always heeded that and left some space, worried I'd confine them in my arms without an exit strategy. Then I felt guilty that maybe I should treat them all the same. Maybe I receded because there were four completely individual sets of needs with kids who came from completely different backgrounds. I didn't want to push them. Deep down, I feared being rejected by my own children.

Even when they'd grown older, maybe especially because they had been older, I was even more sensitive and confused about the boundaries of physical touch. If they had a bad day and needed comfort, should I hug them or rub their backs? Do I just give them their space? If they scored a goal in a soccer game do I hug them or high five? Do I just say, "Great game honey!" Maybe it was all of the above. I was never sure. None of that touching stuff was instinctual for me. I put so much thought into it, then usually felt like I got it wrong. Which made me feel fundamentally flawed as a mother. That stuff was supposed to come naturally. What kind of mother didn't know how to comfort their own child? A shitty one.

I'd never been a cuddly person. I liked my own space. And while I love holding hands with my kids when they reach for mine, I find it weird to hold an adult's hand. It makes me feel like I need rescuing, like I'm a child incapable of getting myself across the street without being run over. Oddly, the night Craig and I first hooked up in Holland, we walked the streets of Arnhem after too many Tequila Sunrises chased by some beers. As we teetered through the streets looking for a late night snack, his pickup line was, "Hold my hand so you don't get lost." I acquiesced, probably out of the youthful naivety of a jaded teenager who didn't yet know she was jaded.

The next morning I assumed he'd already forgotten me so I ignored him and the obvious signs that he really liked me. But he was diligent. Soon I caved to the smart, funny guy who didn't want anything from me but love. So what the hell. I gave it to him. A week and a half later after we'd returned home to the States, he told his mom he'd met the woman he was going to marry. Twenty-something years later, we never held hands anymore because at some point I'd learned exactly how jaded I truly was. And that holding hands made me feel needy, suffocated and confined. Even with a man who only wanted my love.

Outside the confines of my not-so-touchy intimate relationships, I was even worse. My long, awkward, deer-in-the-headlights pauses made greetings and goodbyes painful for both parties. If I could, I avoided saying goodbye altogether by simply disappearing like an apparition. This is my favorite party exit strategy. If I'd met someone new at the party, the next time I saw them I assumed they didn't remember me. Then I'd feel guilty and stupid for bailing on them, which made that next greeting even more uncomfortable than the first. It compounded with every social encounter just like interest.

So that stereotype of the quintessential American hugger? I didn't fit it at all. If I hugged someone, they'd earned it. Probably a million times over. And I'd probably planned to hug them three days ahead of time in order to make it happen. Social kissing? Oh sweet Jesus, you're kidding, right? Kissing as a social greeting messed with my head and screwed with my boundary issues. I didn't do it. 'Cause I was a cultural anomaly, an American freak.

In America there were tons of ways to greet people and choosing the right one caused me tremendous stress. In Morocco, there were only two greetings…the Moroccan way and the French way. There were clear and consistent guidelines for usage that cut out any guesswork. Of course, the French didn't shake hands, which was my impersonal favorite. They kissed. Thank god it wasn't a French kiss. It was hardly a kiss at all. Instead you veered left of the other person's cheek while dryly puckering. Planting it on the cheek was completely unnecessary. Veer right and repeat on the other side. You've seen it before on the *Real Bitchy Housewives of Some Pretentious Big Rich City*, I'm sure. It's also common in smaller cities. Anywhere people are desperately attempting to convince you they're worldly and prefer Camembert over cheddar.

Moroccan greetings were more personal, thoughtful, drawn out and exhausting. Start with the Pledge of Allegiance stance with your right hand over your heart. Then thump your palm like you're giving yourself chest compressions to convey, *you're in my heart.* Already overtly intimate and the greeting hasn't even begun yet. Then there's the accompanying dialogue.

*"Assalam Aleikum. La bas? Kulchi mezien? La ila la bas?"*

In English this means:

"Peace be with you. No problems? Everything is fine? Your family, no problems?"

In America, the correct responses would be:

"Peace, dude. Everything's great! Totally! They're perfect, thanks for asking!"

Those were not the correct answers in Morocco. They wanted the real deal, not the cursory illusion. Do you feel like shit because you have diarrhea? Was your mother just diagnosed with gout? Did your kid get suspended for pulling the fire alarm while pulling down his pants to moon the principal? Yes, you should absolutely mention all these things. It would be rude not to. If you must use this greeting, and you must with all Moroccans except those who work for American companies bred for efficiency like McDonald's, settle in 'cause it could take until noon or beyond. Bring a sandwich.

## FIVE MOROCCAN FAUX PAS

Certain things are just culturally inappropriate. Don't do these things if you want to fit into society and not be considered rude. Or worse, gross. We Americans like our lives to be hygienic and sanitized, and we put our money where our mouth is. We spend billions each year on mouthwash, cleaners, hand sanitizers, tissues, deodorant, air fresheners and vacuum cleaners. Not to mention douches. We'll buy anything that claims to purify the filth that comes with being human. Especially if it comes in the fragrance of fresh cotton. Maybe one day all those products will help clean up our image of being lazy. Until then, we remain a country that really likes lists. So without further ado, here is a list of the top five Moroccan faux pas:

1. Inappropriate Itching and Readjusting. In America, you can scratch your arm, your leg and your ear in public. But we get uncomfortable if someone's finger wanders too close to their nostrils. If someone is scratching their head, we'll be forced to contemplate whether they have dandruff or lice. Of course, it's strictly taboo to touch yourself anywhere your bathing suit covers in public. Every American instinctively knows and follows this unwritten social code. Not so in Morocco. The need to scratch or readjust your junk so it's hanging on your preferred side is equivalent to blinking. Moroccans don't blink when doing it in public.
2. Loogies and Snot Rockets. There is a curious phenomenon in Rabat. On almost every city intersection, someone tries to sell you a box of tissues. The thing is, you never see anyone blowing their noses with one. Tissues are used as napkins or paper towels. It's completely stupid to try to dry your hands with a Kleenex because it pills and you end up with it all over your hands and you still have to wipe your hands on your pants. When Moroccans need to blow their noses, they simply snot rocket that gob o' booger onto the sidewalk. Where it's also acceptable to spit out your loogies. So watch your step.
3. Belching and Farting. Have you ever been by yourself, burped then excused yourself out loud? I have excused myself from myself many a time. That's how ingrained it is in our culture to apologize for natural bodily functions. The rest of the world doesn't see it that way. Or smell it that way, either. So while I'm trying to drill it into my kids' heads not to let it rip in public, the public is ripping away. Corrupting their ideas of proper American social etiquette. We do have to return to the States one day, after all.
4. B.O. and Bad Breath. You are what you eat. Or at least you smell like what you eat. Because so often it stays on your

breath. Especially in Morocco where the cuisine is very onion, garlic and cumin centric. Also dental hygiene is a luxury here, not a matter of national pride like in America. The foods you eat also seep out your pores. Apparently deodorant isn't all that pivotal here socially. Even in the sweltering days of summer when things get really funky. Extremely funky. Which is exacerbated by number five:

5. Crowding and Cutting. While these aren't the grossest faux pas on the list, they are probably the most infuriating to foreigners. In the West we have this notion of personal space. It's as if an invisible bubble surrounds our bodies and protects us, and no one else is allowed to enter it. I mistakenly thought this concept was standard everywhere in the world. It's not. So there is no buffer from bumping, brushing, knocking or being all up in one's space. The social smack-down glare used to counteract it is also a foreign concept. Oh, and cutting the line is the norm, not the exception. Luckily, a firm *la* ("no" in Arabic) with a Jerry Springer finger wave counters that one. Just don't use your middle finger or your thumb.

You may have realized there are more than five social faux pas because I doubled up on each one. So there are actually ten. Because I'm American, I'm just too damn lazy to list them individually. I didn't even mention that Morocco has the world's crappiest toilet paper. That's just a bonus.

*Insert fragrance of fresh cotton here.*

# Chapter 4

# Naked Mission Impossible

It was impossible to be inconspicuous in Morocco. It was a mine-field of cultural traps. Our mission as expats was to blend in, live the local life, and avoid being targeted by American haters. The truth was we were more likely to be in harm's way in America than in Morocco, the third-friendliest place on earth according to the World Economic Forum. America ranked a measly and acrimonious 102nd. Let's face it, we'd given the world plenty of really good reasons to hate us even before Paris Hilton came along.

Even though it was unlikely that anyone would stalk us and chop off our limbs and serve us up in a "beef" and fried green tomato tagine, we still needed to be cautious. It was way more likely that we'd victims of a boring non-violent hate crime like cyberterrorism. In which a hacker would change my Facebook status to something passive-aggressive. *Loving Morocco! Except for the stray mangy cats. Do they know I'm CIA and was sent on a secret mission to implant IUDs and liberate them from fleas? By the way, my bank pin code is 1234.*

American expats were commonly suspected of being spies. And after the elements saw *Spy Kids*, I think they were hopeful that Craig and I were spies and that our car could secretly turn into a submarine. Obviously we weren't spies. The CIA didn't use antiquated flip phones that constantly ran out of minutes because they relied on phone cards bought at Marjane, the Moroccan equivalent of Walmart except way crappier. If you can even imagine that. So obviously I wasn't in the espionage business unless I was really deep undercover.

Even though we weren't spies sent by Bob Barker to spay and neuter Morocco's feral cats, we were obviously American. So many clues gave us away. Our exotic Caucasian-ness was giftwrapped in the national uniform of torn jeans and Nike sneakers, we fidgeted restlessly in long unorganized lines, spoke loudly and slowly in English to people who didn't understand it and bought large amounts of cheddar cheese with a parade of towheaded kids in tow. Except Sky, who considered himself extremely lucky to be a brunette with an olive skin tone so that his ethnicity would be enigmatic anywhere in the world.

Around town, the biggest giveaway to our nationality was our minivan. Moroccans didn't drive minivans and European expats were too sophisticated to drive anything so unchic and fuel inefficient. If that wasn't enough, our yellow diplomatic license plates with the country code 17 in a sea of white ones further confirmed our nationality. Moroccans had broken the secret diplomatic country code numbers with the decoder rings found in the bottom of their Friday night mountain of couscous. That's a lie. The only thing at the bottom of a huge platter of couscous was a pool of olive oil and butter.

It was a major miracle to arrive wherever we were going on the narrow, savage, cratered streets. This really was the place where the streets had no name that Bono sang about. Because most roads didn't have signage, many times the locals didn't even know their names. And pulling over with a map to ask a Moroccan where we were didn't work 'cause most didn't read maps well. Getting around was done by landmarks. Which tends to be how women drivers navigate. They notice small details like the white gate that looks exactly the same as every other one had an unusually large rosemary bush out front to clearly differentiate it from all the others. Which meant the medina would be on the left after we'd passed under the archway with the missing brick.

Although it might sound like driving was women friendly, it wasn't. The majority of drivers were male. Men who didn't read maps or subtle details proficiently. I don't know if there's any correlation between testosterone, excessively caffeinated, sugary Moroccan tea consumption, and the high rate of traffic fatalities in Morocco. It's my hypothesis there truly might have been.

As a foreign woman who used turn signals, stopped at stop signs, used the friendly wave, allowed other cars to merge, respected pedestrian right of way and underutilized the horn, it didn't take long to realize that I was actually far more likely to cause an accident. Culturally, no one there understood driving in an orderly fashion. It was a foreign concept. So to survive in that man-eat-man environment, I needed to become one of the testosterone savages.

Driving that way in the States would have propagated more road rage than we already claimed. I didn't even get what Americans had to rage about on the road. After all, the roads were luxuriously wide, clean, and smoothly paved. We never had a stop sign and a stop light at the same intersection so as to be forced to consider which trumped the other or if you had to stop at all. We had green arrows in the left turn lane to stop traffic from the other direction, for god's sake. And we never had to dodge a goat on the highway. Yet there was always some jackass with a gun in his car who wasn't afraid to use it if the guy in front didn't pull over to the right to let him pass fast enough.

That shit didn't happen in Morocco. The worst that came of a traffic scuffle was an old-fashioned slap and spit fight. There was nothing quite like seeing two grown men get off their mopeds in the middle of traffic after being cut off. To settle it like men with their hands. Slapping, spitting and shouting "*Hmar!*" (Arabic for donkey) in each other's faces. Sure, they temporarily impeded the flow of traffic, as did the crowd that formed to watch the noble gladiators fight until death. Actually the brawl was over when someone's arm got tired or when they heard the call to prayer and remembered it was time to gather their prayer rugs and head to Mosque. Then they got back on their mopeds and it was over. Done. No harm, no foul.

Not only didn't the drivers have guns, the traffic cops weren't even armed. Unless you counted their whistles. Yes, whistles, like the ones used by football referees. Those. So the dogs obeyed the traffic laws because they were the only ones who could hear the high pitched tweets through the incessant honking of car horns. By the way, there were only about three dogs in Morocco but none of them turned right on red. Most traffic cops didn't have a police vehicle or a privately owned car, either. Which was why we frequently saw uniformed police officers hitchhiking to and from work on the back of a moped hugging the male driver. Without a helmet.

If a cop blew the whistle and pointed at your car and you conjured up enough respect to stop, chances were about 50-50 you would be expected to offer a bribe to make the charges disappear. The officer was starting a slush fund to buy his own car or put shoes on his kids' feet because being a cop didn't pay well. After being stopped the first time, you learned it was better, cheaper, more efficient and socially acceptable to not stop. Unless you were feeling charitable. Really the most altruistic thing you could do was to stay in the flow of traffic gripping the steering wheel and trying your best to arrive alive. Doing so was always a major miracle. Thank Allah, Jesus, Buddha or someone else.

My driving metamorphosis happened instantaneously. It was my dream come freakin' true—roller derby with a car. I'd always wanted to drive that way in the States and sometimes had. I loved the adrenaline rush that came with unstructured, chaotic traffic. I loved rebelling against rules that were arbitrary and stupid like speed limits. I was going to get where I was going even if I had to lap the same block ten or more times to do it. No one, not even a pedestrian, was going to stop me.

While I had found one thing to love about Morocco, the unpredictable nature of traffic and life in general stressed the elements. They had culture shock. Sky, who was on the cusp of middle school, had the worst case by far. He was constantly unhappy, moody, and prone to sudden outbursts that usually didn't make any sense. That was his job, and the calling of preteens everywhere, to make every person he was related to miserable. And he took his job seriously. Add to that the interminable Morocco smackdowns and infinite cultural questions he couldn't help but contemplate out loud, all day, every day, and it was the 7th layer of hell.

"Who came up with the name couscous anyway?" "Don't they know it's unsafe to have a family of four riding on one moped at the same time?" "Why is the call to prayer five times a day and why does the guy on the loudspeaker sound like a goat when he sings?" "Why does the French school have a half day every Wednesday?" "Why does the meat here smell like butt?" "Really, you expect me to eat this when it smells like butt?" "Can we move back to Colorado now?"

I guess I couldn't blame him, or I shouldn't. Although I totally did because explaining then re-explaining all this when he forgot the answer thirty seconds later was exhausting. Inevitably, one of the three other elements would arrive mid-explanation and demand to know the secrets we were keeping from them. It was a continuous vicious cycle.

I was too consumed sympathizing with myself to have leftovers enough to sympathize with him. Even though sometimes his grievances were valid. It's gotta be hard to be the minority at a new school in a new country with a new language students weren't supposed to speak at school but did. Where do you think he learned the correct context and pronunciation of *hmar*? In addition, he was completely deprived because he didn't have a driver and a nanny to co-raise him or provide him with all the junk food and video games he'd ever wanted. That must really have sucked.

Unfortunately, he got stuck with parents who loved him enough to force him to live without indulgences. To make matters worse, we forced him to eat vegetables while trying to teach him integrity. If we could cram that in, that was. Sky's intense *I hate Morocco* campaign started early and showed no signs of stopping. He crusaded relentlessly every morning, afternoon and evening of every day we lived there. Granted he did have it hard with some local tormentors and bullies on the bus and at school. But so did the rest of the elements. Sky just took it more personally than the others.

I coped the way I always did by resorting to fantasies. That the hardships of living in Africa would make the elements realize they should band together and protect each other by using their incredibly annoying superpowers for good just this once. To defeat the bad guys rather than each other. Of course, that didn't happen. The elements continued their familial hate-affair and committed to the love thy enemy approach with their "friends." Which was exactly the opposite of what I told them to do.

That's when things got all Stockholm Syndrome-ish at school. Reverie also made me delusional enough to think that all I needed was patience through this whole character-building process. Only I wasn't patient and often resorted to daydreams about pushing Sky or the most annoying element of the moment in front of an oncoming donkey cart. Just a harmless mommy stress-reliever daydream I visualized when I was really worked up and about to implode. Of course I would never have done such a thing. That's what fantasies are for.

Every night Craig and I conducted lengthy debriefings over the dinner table with the elements. Him arriving home for dinner nearly every night was a new occurrence. The crappy American economy had caused budget cuts, so his expected travels throughout Africa had been cut in half. In Colorado, I'd been a single mom a majority of the time. Helping the kids with homework, feeding them and putting them to bed while Craig worked late most every night because he'd married his work. In Morocco we tag-teamed, spending hours trying to explain the traffic, religion, politics, and the smells in the medina diplomatically. Craig would tag me and take over when it came to questions about medical items or physics.

"The American medical system isn't better," he would say, "it's just different. You have to have health insurance to get medical care back home. In Morocco, you don't need insurance. Everyone is equally entitled to crappy medical care."

"It is possible to balance a family of four on a single moped with both a goat and a ladder. However, the key is to keep the center of gravity low and not try to do it totem-pole style."

My topics of expertise were politics and food.

"No," I would explain, "English royalty and Moroccan royalty are completely different. Queen Elizabeth is a figurehead who doesn't do much but drink tea and wear weird hats. Wait, maybe there are more similarities than I thought. Let me get back to you on that."

"You will eat that eggplant because it's the freshest vegetable at the store now after the drought that caused a massive red pepper fruit fly infestation. And god knows I'm not buying the imported asparagus because shipping it from Europe wastes fossil fuels. Plus we need to stimulate the local Moroccan economy. Now eat it!"

I don't think any of this talking changed how the elements saw anything. But being together every night for a family dinner changed things significantly for me. Craig was home to assist with homework, which had always been a completely overwhelming time of day. Not only would I have to remember the algebra I'd sucked at the first time around, I still had three other kids to prod and help while making dinner. Craig became the math and science tutor. I tackled English, social studies and meals.

When dinner time arrived and the kids whined about how terrible it was…every night…I could look across the table and see another adult eating it without complaint, mouth closed, using a napkin. Appreciative of all the work that went into whatever creation I'd come up with in a bid to emulate fajitas in the absence of tortillas. Unless I made the tortillas from scratch, which I did. Just once. After all the post-dinner squabbles, showering and tucking in, I had someone to rant to and with about what a pain in the ass the elements were over a glass of wine. Until we remembered how much joy they brought us when they were quietly asleep in their beds.

~

Craig's job with the Peace Corps even made taking time off to travel easier. So for spring break we drove three hours south to the hushed beach town of Oualidia for even more family togetherness, if we could stand it. We left the honking Rabat traffic and the colossal Marjane behind. This was the real Morocco, real rural. A couple of mom and pop stores provided the basics along with a local butcher who wouldn't let me photograph the meat hanging fly-ridden in the midday sun. There was no medina or kasbah, only the beach. An inlet boasting languid waves and a sandy, shallow bottom was the perfect place for the elements to learn to surf.

Local fishermen sold the day's catch on the beach. We could ponder how long it'd been out in the sun and how long and unpleasant the journey through our intestines and eventually back out to sea would be. Not that we wanted to. But that's about all there was to do. There was nothing quite like wide open spaces, sand and water to make the elements play together for a few entire minutes all continuous like. Especially after a long road trip during which they had been entertained soley by their contempt for each other because there was no DVD player to distract them.

Amidst the suckage of our first trip, there was one true bonding family moment. A who-has-enough-balls-to-eat-the-fish's-eyeballs contest over the dinner I cooked in the condo's tiny kitchen. Turned out that everyone but me would eat a fish eye. I only drank Fish Eye from the box. Which you couldn't get there.

After we got the first trip out of the way, it was all on. A couple months later we drove down South to Marrakech, the most touristy city in all of Morocco. Where I got assaulted by a henna lady who appeared out of nowhere and started performing random acts of henna on my hand. When she was done two seconds later, she charged me $30 for her unfinished, improvised handiwork. She thought I was a stupid American who'd fall for her scam. Americans are smarter than that. We invented scams, so your typical American would refuse to pay to be molested and stained. Since I'm half Canadian. I paid her $15. Then I felt guilty that maybe I should have given her $20.

While I was consumed by what a reprehensible person I was for only paying half the asking price, Sky felt that his American righteousness was totally justified. The snake charmers in the square who draped cobras across the shoulders of unsuspecting tourists might have helped. They wouldn't remove the snakes until they got paid. Luckily they accepted dirham, dollars and Euros. Although there might have been an additional service charge for the inconvenience of having to go to the bank to exchange currencies.

We had become well-versed in Morocco's ways by the time we took our first trip across the Strait of Gibraltar. It was summer, and we boarded the ferry to Spain. Europe with its foreign clean streets and orderly traffic. Where pedestrians had the right of way and I needed to chant that in my head so I didn't charge my car at the promenading Spaniards like a bull. It had become so habitual to thank people with a cursory *merci* that we kept correcting ourselves with, "Oops, I mean gracias." We gorged on pork and Rioja. We mixed in some vegetables every now and again because Europeans, like Americans, appreciated a crisp lettuce salad. Especially when it was topped with pork products like bacon. We'd been deprived of both for too long.

"It's so disturbing!" the boys exclaimed.

We were on the beach where most of the women were topless. In Morocco topless meant going out without a headscarf. There it meant that total strangers knew if you had saucer nipples, implants, a bad Tweety Bird tattoo on your rack, wore a padded bra or should. While Moroccan women were draped and covered like a statue of the Virgin Mary, Spanish women dressed more like Mutha Mary, fictional gangsta rap artist. Skirts that barely covered their asses had been paired with skimpy halter tops and really fashionably foot-tormenting stripper shoes. And that counted as being completely clothed before stripping down to a thong on the beach. Only a thong.

Then they played paddle ball in the waves. It's impossible not to watch a topless game of any sport even if the women were seventy-five with mastectomy scars and every morsel of your being screamed for you to look away. For better or worse, it was simply hypnotizing. Our necks were more sore than if we'd watched an intense Wimbledon match. The boys were so disturbed they couldn't sleep at night just thinking about it. Unless that was the neck pain.

Jade, on the other hand, was horrified by the public display of boobs on parade. At nine, she knew her set would be coming in at some point. "Mine aren't gonna be big like that, are they?" she asked. "I want small ones. Like you have, mom."

Which marked the first time anyone had ever envied my starter boobs.

"Unfortunately," I said, "they aren't made to order. You get what you get and you don't throw a fit."

I'm sure I said something a bit kinder and gentler, more tailored to her sensitive nature. Ember was the one who didn't understand subtleties but she was too busy snaking her arm under her one-piece swimsuit to mound wet sand on her chest to overhear our conversation.

Jade required a gentler approach to make up for the fact that her brother violated her innocence by informing her where babies came from several years before…much too early for her to learn the harsh reality.

"Babies," he told her, "are made when a boy pees inside a girl and the baby has to get cut out."

He heard that at school and couldn't wait to share the excitingly grotesque details with his siblings. It was the only thing they enjoyed sharing with each other…gross, gossipy half-truths. I had to do damage control before it trickled down the ranks and reached Ember.

"Sometimes," I said, "a baby doesn't need to be cut out. Sometimes it just rips the vagina open on its own."

I said that because I believe in natural birth control fueled by harsh realities. The boys needed to bear the burden of their choices too, so I made sure to terrify them by saying, "When you have a baby you can't do anything you want to for the next eighteen years so you can take care of it. You definitely won't be able to afford an X-box or have time to play it. Oh, wait. Who am I kidding? In today's economy it's at least thirty years."

~

When we returned home, we were greeted by a phone call from one of Craig's colleagues. This woman was one of the most untactful, direct people I'd ever met. She was so matter-of-fact and flat in her emotional tone I suspected she was a robot. When Craig answered, she immediately passed the phone to a stranger. This stranger was an American expat named Kim who was at the garage sale of another expat. I know that because only foreigners had garage sales. It was the only place we could find coveted often broken American and European items not sold in Morocco or boxes of expired Jell-O.

That's how I made my first friend. Through a robot at a garage sale. And how I ended up naked in front of strangers.

## SPAGHETTI

I'm not a girl who frequents the spa. I've only been three times in my life, to use up gift cards given to me by people who mustn't have known me very well. Maybe they were really trying to give me a hint. It's not that I'm unhygienic, I'm just a do-it-yourself, clip-and-go, no-frills kinda girl. The way my mother was before me. You know, practical. Until my new friend Kim invited me to *hammam* with her.

*Hammam* is a Turkish bath house where you get steamed, showered and scrubbed by a complete stranger in front of other total strangers while you're stark naked. Even though I'd only known Kim a few weeks, I thought we were ready to take our friendship to the next level. Because in the expat world everything moved faster, which was clearly why we were ready to bridge nakedness and public humiliation together.

We headed down the stairs into the basement past the pool to the entrance. Where we were greeted by *hammam* lady who gestured that it was time for us to get naked. Already? We just got there. She waited while we undressed, took our clothes and led us to the steam room. Where we were supposed to relax and not panic because it was so hot and steamy it was hard to breathe. All while looking casual talking to your friend and trying not to let your eyes wander.

When we were adequately pruned, the attendant returned and slathered us with a salve of something that looked like cat diarrhea. She applied it liberally all over our bodies. And *yes*, I mean *all* over. In a militant, no-body-part-left-behind kind of way. Apparently there was no cultural taboo about touching where a bikini covers cause she was all up in that junk. (Not that I have junk, just to clarify that.) Once marinated and simmering in poo, I mean goo, it was time to head to the marble slab in the other room. Lying naked on a slab in a basement was a bit eerie and morgue-ish. Except it smelled better. And it was heated.

She took the sprayer and rinsed me off head to toe. It was weird to have someone else do something I was perfectly capable of doing myself. Yet oddly comforting at the same time. Then she pulled out the scrubber. Which was a mitt of stiff nylon nubs, essentially a heavy duty kitchen scouring pad. She started on my back and was anything but gentle. After she'd been at it for a while, she showed me the long rolls of dead skin she pulled out of the clogged scrubber and scrunched up her nose.

"Spaghetti," she said then laughed.

I would have called them dreadlocks. Anyway, I was completely embarrassed by how utterly disgusting I was. Why hadn't anyone told me how gross I was before? I must have lost a whole two pounds of skin. And another two pounds of water weight in the steam room.

When I glanced at the next slab over, Kim's freshly scrubbed back was as red as the mitt. Then it was time to turn over. To do the front side. Yes, the front. Some parts of a woman's body should never come into contact with anything abrasive, by American standards, anyhow. My nipples might never recover.

At that point, I was too raw to care what she did next. Which was a series of awkward leg stretches followed by instructions for me to lie on my stomach and stretch my arms over my head. She grabbed them and slid my body back and forth. If the goal was to make me laugh hysterically, mission accomplished. She finished by putting a mask of honey on my face and left me lying sunny side up with cucumber slices over my eyes. I really could have used some on my nipples and crotch.

I was sure *hammam* lady had forgotten all about me when she finally reappeared bearing a robe and reunited me with my clothes and Kim. Sure, I'd lost my humility but I'd gained a friend and really tough nipples for life.

## HAMMAM PREPAREDNESS CHECKLIST

1. You don't have that recurrent nightmare you're naked in public anymore.
2. The sight of cat diarrhea does not make you vomit.

3. You like it a little rough.
4. In fact, *Hurts So Good* is one of your favorite songs.
5. You wanted to lose five pounds anyway.
6. A steamy basement room without windows doesn't make you claustrophobic.
7. You never met a Slip and Slide you didn't like.
8. Your friendship knows no bounds. Or boundaries.
9. You don't have *Private: No Trespassing* tattooed on your bikini line.
10. You passed a nipple sensitivity test with your kitchen scouring pad.

# Chapter 5

## Girlfriends, Lesbians, and Men's Cafe

Kim and I were instantly thick as thieves. She was in Rabat on a year-long sabbatical from her law practice with her husband and two kids. She came from Boulder, a mere hour and a half north of our place in the States. So we were neighbors who traveled to Africa to meet each other.

I couldn't help but wonder if we'd have become friends if we'd met stateside because we were opposites in almost every way. She was a working professional, I was gainfully unemployed. She liked baking, I liked cooking. She liked sweets, I preferred salt. She was logical and analytical while I unfortunately was not. What we did have in common was that we were both goofballs always up for an adventure, especially if it involved combining the two. I missed my girlfriends so badly it was good to make one there. Someone who seemed to understand me and enjoy my off-the-beaten-path take on life.

Kim only had five more months before she would move back home. We were determined not to waste time doing stupid stuff. Instead, we completely committed ourselves to it. We hung out most days with a glass of ice tea pondering the cultural differences in our homes away from home and how thankful we were to be Western women who could do almost anything we wanted besides become priests. Not that we wanted to be priests. Luckily, our husbands and kids also got along famously. Even so, I wanted and needed to make more friends.

This was the one time when it was great that expats were so easily identifiable. Most of them spoke English, which was why they were my potential friend pool. When you're deprived of hearing English, you develop this superior bat sonar that can detect it two miles away. Striking up a conversation with a complete stranger had never been easier even for this anxious introvert.

What's awesome was we could skip formalities altogether and just start with the thing on every expats mind, food. It was a pragmatic approach. In less than thirty seconds you could sum up everything you need to know about an expat from one very important question: *If bugs are in the cornmeal you just bought, do you make cornbread and eat it anyway*? The correct answer was yes. Any other answer, including *I don't like cornbread*, meant you were a hostile elitist and not worth investing my time.

While I usually disregard organized associations of any kind out of sheer contempt for social order and mandatory dues, I was a bit desperate. Which was why I initially read the invitation for an International Women's Association to be held at the American Ambassador's house the following week. Bingo. That was my target audience. They were international. They were women. They spoke English. So I ignored my social phobia and decided I had to do this. All that was left was to find a suitable dress that said *confident worldly woman* and wear it for an hour. Although an hour was completely pushing my acting skills to the limit.

I met the U.S. Ambassador Samuel Kaplan and his wife Sylvia, who looked like an older, pre-surgical version of Sharon Osborn if she wore a sleeveless muumuu exposing side boob through the armholes.

After the initial pleasantries, which I found unpleasant and blundering on my part, I lingered my way through the house to check out the décor's accents heavy handed in orange, my favorite color. Back on the patio I was transported to America, complete with iced tea with abundant ice surrounded by the din of small talk in English. The women were split about 60/40 with the ball in the Moroccan court. I sat at a table where I was the token American. But everyone was already engrossed in conversation, so I had to unskillfully create my own.

I headed to the buffet where I tried to make meaningful conversation. "Your headscarf is beautiful. Is it an antique?"

What was I saying? Scarves couldn't be antiques. The word was vintage, dumbass.

"These cookies are delicious. Are they made with almonds and honey? Both. Wow. I never would have guessed." Except yes, I would have because all the freakin' cookies in the country contain almonds and honey. For the love of god, shove some food into your mouth you buffoon and make the pathetic attempt at small talk end.

Back on the patio, I boldly approached two European women in their fifties. They were friendly, toned and articulate. Making conversation with them was easy because they carried it. I just kept asking questions. They worked for the same nonprofit organization, lived in Mali, and travelled extensively throughout Africa together. I was intrigued with what life must have been like for a lesbian couple on a continent where it was illegal to be gay. A lull in the conversation provided an opportunity to ask.

"How great that you two get to travel the world together as a couple!" I said knowingly. Right before a confused pause. The taller, tanner, more dominant lesbian shook her head.

"No, no, no." They began a synchronized scramble for words. "Our husbands blah, blah, blah."

I guess my gaydar didn't work in Africa. It wouldn't be the last time, either.

~

When we returned from a family trip to Tuscany that August, Kim said an exercise class was starting the following day. The instructor was an American woman, a former professional dancer, and her advertisement promised no running. That was all Kim and I needed to hear. We arranged to meet at the park because I would show up right after a super-secret covert therapy session with Craig and Emma. We weren't disclosing our marital troubles to any of our friends for fear it would make hanging out with us uncomfortable for them.

At the end of that session, we discussed how Craig and I couldn't have a meaningful conversation about our relationship because I abruptly and unintentionally fell asleep. That's when Emma said it.

"I've heard of this before. And everything you're telling me fits together and makes perfect sense."

Really? It did? 'Cause it didn't make any sense to me.

"It's textbook," she said.

I was textbook? Synonymous with predictable, complacent, expected and boring.

She confirmed my previous therapist's diagnosis that I was codependent and that I avoided emotional confrontations by falling asleep. Just the way a child cried themselves to sleep after a twenty minute temper tantrum. Except I wasn't a child. I didn't cry or have temper tantrums because I internalized anything negative while ignoring everything positive. When things got stressful, codependents unwittingly sought out chaos, turmoil and distractions. Check. Check. And check. So, maybe I was textbook after all.

The session came with a new homework assignment. To walk through the park together before Craig went to work and I worked out. We had fifteen minutes until class started…coincidentally at the park near Emma's house. At the entrance I saw a strikingly fit and beautiful woman whose eyes resembled Jennifer Anniston's. Except she was a dead ringer for Princess Lalla Salma, the wife of Mohammed VI, King of Morocco. Sitting on the bench in the park sporting spandex pants and comfortable sneakers sans tiara.

"Hi. You must be Sara," I said acting super casual.

"I am." Her response was accompanied by a huge, all-American smile.

"I'm Marie and this is my husband Craig." And we hadn't just come from couples therapy, in case you were wondering.

"It's nice to meet you." She knew, didn't she?

"I'm coming to your class today. We're just going to, um, take a quick walk around the park. And I'll be right back." 'Cause we were so romantic that we walked every day at 9:45 a.m. because that's the time we met exactly twenty-something years ago.

That's total bullshit, by the way.

The only person in town besides us who knew that was Emma. Who stood next to me in her workout clothes. She knew some intimate things about us but I really didn't know anything about her. And I definitely hadn't met athletic Emma before. So pretending to meet her for the first time wasn't too hard. Not sharing with Kim how awkwardly hilarious this whole scene was killed me. I was tempted to brownnose with Emma. *Did you see us doing our homework? Do I get an A in therapy now?* But, I refrained.

Instead Kim and I giggled through Sara's workout out of squats, more squats, then lunges, firmly establishing ourselves as the disruptive asses of the class. Who would soon have very tight asses.

~

A couple weeks later, we were invited to tour a local winery with a young power couple we'd just met. She looked like Tea Leoni, and his boyish good looks made him the most lusted after male expat in town.

We were fast approaching our first Ramadan in a Muslim country. During the holy month, there was no eating during the day, no smoking, no sex, no drinking and no swearing. Which translated meant, *it fucking sucks*. Even though Muslims weren't supposed to drink, Morocco had wineries. Plural. And they produced millions of bottles every year. It must have been for export I thought. But, have you ever seen Moroccan wine in a store near you? Probably not because 80% of it was consumed in Morocco. Where 99% of the population was Muslim. You do the math. In other words, it's the equivalent of Catholics and premarital sex. Except, the Catholics win that one by a landslide. So never mind.

The answer was, we needed to get some spirits, holy or not, right away before the locals did. When Ramadan started, the whole country went dry and we couldn't buy any alcohol for a whole thirty days straight.

As we were leaving, our friends ran into work colleagues of theirs and introduced us. Those acquaintances introduced us to their friends who they'd brought along. That's how I met Monique. A lithe yoga instructor who moved to Northern Morocco from Canada with her husband and two young daughters just days before. We stood outside of the winery on a balmy Moroccan day and talked for quite a while. Enough to ascertain she was friendly, bubbly but not annoyingly so, intelligent and engaging. Someone I could be friends with who got the Canadian in me. Before we said goodbye we exchanged e-mails.

Monique travelled back to Tangier, her new home, and we wrote to each other. We had a lot in common. We commiserated about having left our girlfriends behind and discovered we had a mutual love of writing. She had a way of getting right to the point and cutting out all the bullshit I hated. There were no conversations about the weather or sports. Instead it was spirituality and politics. We clicked right from the beginning.

A couple weeks later she returned to Rabat briefly during Ramadan. We arranged to meet at a local café where we had a deep, meaningful discussion about her Algerian roots. How she'd been raised in the West and how Moroccans misperceived her. We lingered in the empty bistro in the middle of the afternoon over our cafe au laits and croissants with jam.

When she returned to town a couple weeks after that, I invited her and her family over for dinner. She said her plans had changed and that she would arrive later in the evening than expected. Since Craig was in Swaziland, we couldn't meet at a restaurant or club because I didn't have anyone to watch the elements. I suggested she stop at my house for a glass of wine after our collective kids were in bed.

The conversation was as effortless as the last two times. For the first two hours. Until without warning, something changed and she got weird. Even though the conversation was the same, her energy was completely different. I couldn't put my finger on it, so I convinced myself it was in my head. I kept trying to think of ways to end our conversation politely and call it a night. It went on for another uncomfortable hour. OK, two.

In the early morning hours, she finally grew tired and I walked her out the front gate to her car. That's where she kissed me. Not a kiss intended for my cheek but missed the target. Not a friendly kiss. A passionate, let-me-throw-you-on-the-bed kind of kiss. Stunned and speechless, I searched for anything I might have said to lead her to believe I was interested in her in that way, but found nothing.

Just to make sure I hadn't misunderstood her intentions, she said, "Let's try that again."

Then kissed me a second time.

That's when I kissed our friendship goodbye.

~

OK, so maybe there was something to that codependency thing. Because anytime I've ever felt an overwhelmingly instant and familiar bond with someone I've just met, it's because they're emotional vampires. Their crazy ass fucked up wants combined with my crazy ass fucked up need to give them exactly what they want, when they want it with a smile on my face explained some of my prior toxic relationships. Ones that made me feel empty and worthless because I was a pawn. My lack of self-esteem had been the only invitation necessary. It was my inbred character flaw, to be nice, no matter the cost to me. Looking back, it all made sense. Now, as counterintuitive as it sounds, I know to stay away from anyone I feel an overwhelming instant chemistry with.

I starting reading everything on the internet about codependency, narcissists, toxic people, emotional vampires, sociopaths, body language, marriage and divorce. Anything that would provide insight into how to recognize and avoid those people so I wouldn't lay out the welcome mat for them to enter my life again. That was the first thing I knew I needed. I needed to get healthy. Also, I wanted women in my life. Ones who liked me for me, not for what I could get them. And who would never try to kiss me. More than that, I wanted to know what it meant to be a woman on a much grander scale. Prompting me to carry out my first social experiment.

## IT'S A MAN'S WORLD

On the bustling streets of Rabat, I couldn't help but notice all the street-side cafes. On second glance, I realized none of those cafes had any female patrons. The customers were all men gathered in packs sipping their coffee and Moroccan tea imbibing in man talk. That got me to thinking. How much would it shake things up when two women in business attire infiltrated their turf? Better yet, could we get a shoeshine boy to work his magic on our inadequately feminine shoes? I and my partner in crime Kim were about to test the waters. Let the social experiment begin.

Now, I hadn't worked in over ten years so I dug deep into my closet's recesses to find work clothes and dust off my heels. I wasn't sure I could even walk in pumps after all those years of comfortable mom shoes, and the killer workout yesterday made me doubt even more. Although I didn't miss working, I did miss the opportunity to dress up now and again.

Kim, who was on sabbatical from being a bona fide professional, wasn't so stoked about the dressing professionally part. It was her year to wear comfortable mom shoes. I picked her up and we searched for just the right testosterone-filled cafe. There were so many to choose from. We found a bright, sunny spot at the corner of two busy streets that was absolutely packed with men, about fifteen tables worth. Not a woman in sight.

We casually sat at a table. All the men in the cafe were speaking Darija. Kim was positive we were the topic of conversation. We had the benefit of not knowing because neither of us spoke the language but we did get interminable glares. And really, if you've never been to a country where staring is perfectly acceptable, there was no three-second rule. They could maintain the visual assault as long as they liked. I can't even express how acutely uncomfortable it was to be unapologetically stared at or precisely how vulgar and malicious someone can be with their eyes.

We ordered coffee from the waiter. Who begrudgingly returned with them. We caught up on life's events since we'd last seen each other. Then Kim mentioned that she'd heard knees were the erotic equivalent of boobs in Morocco. Sitting down made my dress creep up my thighs an inch or two to fully expose my knees. As if things weren't uncomfortable enough, now I'm sitting at an all-male cafe topless with my knees exposed. Even that wasn't getting us any shoeshine action. Maybe my knees weren't big enough. Although they were quite perky.

Kim knew of another cafe where we could score some shoeshine action. It was smaller and more secluded but it was packed nonetheless. We order some frou-frou European bubbly water and were briefly distracted by a guy selling bootleg DVDs. It was the first time I'd been told a DVD was in English and it actually was. Not that I would know for sure or anything for those of you who might work with the FBI.

Then we spotted him crossing the street with his little wooden box. We got an adrenaline rush and made eye contact. He acknowledged us. Unless he was acknowledging our money. Either way, we negotiated a price and voila, Kim was getting her boots shined. Followed by my high heels. I wonder if that's the first time he'd shined a stiletto. I know for sure it was the first time I'd had my shoes removed by a man who wasn't getting anything other than the privilege of shining my shoes. Besides a great view of my knees and the wafting fumes of my very ripe feet.

After having scored the shoeshine guy, Kim and I craved a cigarette. Oh, you know what I mean. It just seemed like the natural way to finish an afternoon of hours spent doing nothing but drinking coffee, shooting the shit with shiny shoes, and visually assaulting people. When it was all over, I was surprised we'd been successful. I couldn't help wondering if we would have gotten a different reaction if we'd been Moroccan and had known Darija and what the men were saying. Instead, we were protected by our foreignness and cultural irrelativism. I wonder how different the experience would have been if I'd worn a burka?

# Chapter 6

## Delusions of Africa

When we'd first moved to Morocco, I had all these delusions of grandeur. I was going to speak French fluently. The kids were going to love and appreciate my cooking. I was going to help the less fortunate. Not become them because we couldn't speak French and communicate with the butcher. And we were going to travel to remote African countries like Rhodesia. Except there was a big problem; it didn't exist anymore. One of my many problems was I daydreamed too much and researched too little, especially where travel was concerned.

Things I didn't know about inter-Africa travel before we moved to Morocco:

1. It's ridiculously expensive to buy one airline ticket, let alone six. So we could take a trip to Ghana but I'd have to sell one of the elements on the black market. OK, I'd have to sell all the elements just to buy two tickets.
2. Ridiculously expensive flights to crazy remote places only have one flight in and out in a week. Bye, bye Gabon.
3. Getting there will require some kind of convoluted connection somewhere totally out of the way. Likely involving leaving

Africa, connecting to a flight in Europe or Dubai only to end up back in Africa, hopefully at our destination. That tripled the travel time and required countless bags of pretzels to be eaten just because they were there. And do you know how many plastic cups full of precisely two ounces of soda we would waste? Lots.

4. This ridiculously expensive, once a week flight to Togo through Dubai that wasted at least four plastic cups would inevitably leave at 2 a.m. Even though it was the middle of the night, the pretzels would still be eaten because they're there. It's true, you know it is!
5. Upon arrival in Togo, there was absolutely nothing to do. Which was the point in the first place. But now you're childless and bored in Togo. Congratulations!

Craig traveled to those remote, exotic destinations sans family on the government's dime for work. While he jetted off to Tanzania, Gambia, Cameron, Togo, Benin and Senegal, the kids and I stayed home and did homework. Which wasn't as fun as it sounded and wasn't why we'd come to Africa. So we had to plan B it. Plan B-ing was a recurrent theme with us.

The Peace Corps had almost three hundred volunteers in Morocco alone. In addition to the hundreds of other volunteers from fourteen different West African countries who sometimes traveled to Rabat for healthcare. Lonely, young Peace Corps workers visiting the big city all alone with no place to go. That was it! Let the sickos bring the African experience and hopefully not some extremely rare contagion to us!

Volunteers lived in tiny villages, spoke the local language, ate the local foods, froze in the mountains in the winter, scorched in the desert in summer. They were more than a little deprived of the American way of life and often were legitimately depressed. They only wanted the simple things. Heat, clean water, a home-cooked meal, and native English speakers to tell their stories to.

I'd always wanted to feed the starving children in Africa. I just didn't know the vast majority would be twenty-three years old with a bachelor's degree in psychology or liberal arts and American. It was the perfect symbiotic relationship. We had them over and enjoyed a whole night of their stories of grit, grime and adventure. We provided them with heat, a home-cooked meal and a captive audience of four kids who thought they were cooler than Justin Bieber. Not that the elements knew who he was or that he wasn't cool at all.

The volunteers appreciated everything and anything we did for them because they'd been completely on their own without a microwave and therefore didn't take anything for granted. They didn't whine and they ate my food, even having seconds or thirds. Then they told stories and patiently answered the elements' questions for hours on end. They were the perfect guests, except they usually hadn't bathed in quite a while. Which was also a great hygiene reminder for the elements.

The elements hiked Kilimanjaro, taught Cameroonian children English, procured a prosthetic leg for a young boy who's real one got blasted off in a firecracker accident, evacuated from Niger after a kidnapping, and cleaned countless water sources simply by urging the locals not to let farm animals defecate in it. All without leaving our house.

After the elements reluctantly went to bed, Craig and I heard the grittier stories. Mostly from female volunteers. It was usually something like they went to check their e-mail at an internet cafe where a local man unzipped his pants, pulled out his penis and masturbated in public while staring at her. That was what being a foreign female do-gooding alone in rural Africa frequently got you—repeatedly sexually violated. Even in big city of Rabat, sexual harassment wasn't uncommon.

~

We would have loved to have taken four appreciative volunteers on our next adventure but we took the unappreciative elements instead. We rode the ferry across the Strait of Gibraltar to see all 2.5 square miles of the rock. It was the worst the British had to offer in a confined space shared with feral monkeys who also called it home. If you love greasy, salty fish and chips you can eat in your tiny, overpriced hotel room complete with a shared bathroom down the hall where one can easily contract warts, it might be your dream destination. Our dream was to go to an English territory to get the elements their first professional non-mom haircuts by someone who spoke English. Which of course the local hairdressers didn't because they were Spanish and drove over the border to Gibraltar for work.

One trip, four shitty Spanish haircuts that weren't any better than mine, and one taste of Yorkshire pudding was enough to last a lifetime. We were home in plenty of time to experience our first Eid, one of several Muslim holidays when everything closes. Everything. At least there was a hiatus on burning garbage on holidays. Because garbage was burned in the plastic garbage bags. Not to worry, though. A few years ago they banned black trash bags and opted for the obviously less toxic green plastic bags. Clearly, green plastic was better for the environment.

Another Eid would happen the next month. There was always another one. This was the one where they killed a sheep or a goat and roasted it in an open field used as a garbage dump. Double bonus! Cook the goat and burn the garbage at the same time. They smelled the same, anyway.

Eid was kinda like Christmas in that we were voluntarily required to give gifts to everyone so they could get their goat. Literally. We found out about this tradition when the garbage man rang our doorbell at 2 a.m. Speaking Darija to Craig, who understood a bit of it in the middle of the day but not in the middle of the night. He had no idea what they wanted until after he got them to leave. The garbage dude wanted his Eid bonus. And we'd stiffed him. Not that the garbage men deserved a bonus because the vast majority of the garbage blew through the streets of Rabat.

On a regular day, the streets offer some crazy sights. Trucks carried cows and three human passengers intermingled with the farm animals. A family of four sandwiched onto a single moped with a single seat. Two guys snuggled on a moped carrying a ladder. Not in a gay snuggly way, though. I thought I'd seen everything Moroccan traffic had to offer until Eid when entire families crammed on a single moped carrying their live goat. And the only one wearing a helmet was the goat. That was going to die in two days' time anyway.

Fortunately, I found a last-minute deal to escape all that. Tickets out of town for the next Eid. I timed the trip precisely to miss the festivities. It was our first African destination as a family outside Morocco. To Egypt. Even the elements were excited.

## CAIRO, UH-OH

I've learned a few things through my travels. Call the credit card company and bank beforehand so they don't freeze your accounts thinking you've stolen your own card. And second, nothing ever goes as planned. Ever.

Ever started when we arrived at the airport in Cairo about 6:00 p.m. and presented our passports at customs. Egyptian guy scanned our official passports and asked for our official visas. What official visas? Behind us was a kiosk where Americans and Europeans could simply buy a visa. That was, any American not carrying an official passport. So we are shuttled to the waiting area while someone talked to someone else to figure things out.

"Don't worry," we assured the elements. "These things have a way of working themselves out."

The Seven Stages of Grief

1. Denial: We called the US Embassy in Cairo. We were sure the Embassy could talk to the customs people and settle the whole thing. A couple hours later...
2. Pain and Guilt: The Embassy couldn't do anything. Apparently a couple of years ago an Egyptian diplomat tried to enter the U.S. without a—guess what—official visa. And do you think we let him in? Nope. Paybacks are a bitch. And why hadn't we asked anyone whether we would need an official visa? Oh, because who knew there were two different kinds of visas?! The outdated 1996 Fodor's travel guide we borrowed from the Peace Corps library didn't mention any of this.
3. Anger and Bargaining: Some official talked to some other official to figure this mess out while we waited. At least we thought they were talking to each other about this. Then finally one of the customs guys announced, "Don't worry," (wink, wink). He told us to collect our things and escorted us to the doors of the terminal with our luggage and unstamped passports. Did I say almost to the doors of the terminal? Because we got stopped by another set of airport officials and were turned around. Damn it, we were so close! We were extradited to another waiting room that looked like a tent city full of homeless people after a hurricane complete with established territorial spots clearly delineated by luggage, sleeping people, or a big pile of cigarette butts. Although the room was plastered with no smoking signs everyone casually ignored, which probably was best when a large group of unhappy people were confined in a small, mosquito infested room. Which made me wonder: were we supposed to take anti-malarial meds when traveling to Egypt?
4. Depression: We'd resided in tent city for a few hours. We've braided hair, watched the second hand on the clock move, laughed at the old guy snoring on his makeshift bench bed, explained the situation to the elements over and over try-

ing to satiate their queries, bought overpriced airport food and water. Now our mosquito bites are welting up so we look like we have chicken pox. It was late and we resigned ourselves to being stuck and having to find a spot in the airport to sleep. I bet no one wanted to pickpocket the itchy, rashy, contagious looking family asleep on the floor. Unless they were also itchy, rashy and contagious looking from mosquito bites. Dammit!

5. The Upward Turn: Good morning, Starbucks coffee! I couldn't believe they had Starbucks there! Yippee! Their mugs have pictures of the pyramids and the sphinx that we won't be seeing. "Your biggest, strongest coffee and the mugs, please." "What a cute stuffed bleating camel! Four, please." "Do you have that Ankh in silver?" Perfect. Shopping was proceeded by playing the sock game where the kids took off their rank socks and whipped each other. Then they strung the luggage together like trains cars. Then we ate. And ate. And ate. Then I had a fling with Justin Timberlake. He wasn't my first choice but while imprisoned in an airport in Africa I settled for JT (or a large billboard of him). Don't worry. Craig got Kate Moss. Also not on the list. Don't judge us.
6. Reconstruction: After forty hours in the Cairo airport, someone somewhere finally got us on a flight back to Morocco. They told us five minutes before the flight left. At that point we were happy to get out of the airport to go anywhere. And the flight was nonsmoking and mosquito free because they sprayed the aisles with pesticides from aerosol cans just to make sure. And I was worried about breathing the smoke? At least any mosquitos we might have accidentally ingested are now dead.
7. Acceptance and Hope: We arrived home at 9:00 a.m. Monday morning. Craig and Ember's sixth birthday (OK, Craig was a few years older). We celebrated with our exhausted, stinky selves. I couldn't stop thinking that we could still salvage the vacation time. There must have been somewhere

we could go. No. We would go somewhere. I booked a flight and secured a hotel but we still had to get up early to catch the flight out of Casablanca. I switched out the shorts in the luggage for coats, hats and gloves. The next morning, the alarm didn't go off. It was 5:10 a.m. With an hour drive to the airport, there was no way even if everything went perfectly that we could make the 7:10 flight but we were sure gonna try.

# Chapter 7

# Holiday Stress

Just the day before we'd been diplomatic inmates at the Cairo airport. In less than twenty-four hours we'd gone from being captives in Egypt, deported to Morocco, eating birthday cake in our museum house, booking a new trip only to wake up late and plow through red lights on Mr. Toad's Wild Ride to the Casablanca airport. We were all sleep-deprived with souvenir mosquito bites from terminal two.

The harrowing journey ended in Paris. Thanksgiving in the city of romance. If we hadn't been traveling with four kids, all of whom shared the single hotel room intended for an occupancy of three. Rebooking our plans for Paris had been a bit insane, especially considering we'd blown a few thousand dollars on a stay-cation at the airport in Cairo. So now, instead of seeing the great pyramids, the sphinx and the Nile covered in sunshine, we were surrounded by the Eiffel tower, the Arc de Triumph and the damp gloom that kicked off the long, dark European winter.

Despite the depressing weather, Paris had an aura of magic. The wafting smell of baguettes filled the streets every morning. The sidewalks were crammed with fashionable, petite pedestrians walking efficiently yet effortless. Their hands gestured and flourished alluringly, somehow making smoking an elegant and chic performance art. In complete contrast to the way Moroccans smoked. They dragged with intent and purpose. There was no style involved, only the urgent need for a fix.

The French had a way of looking ambivalent about everything. They didn't have a need for needs or at least made it look like they didn't. In that culture, it was more important to keep up the appearance that they were completely self-sufficient and haughty. So it might not come as a surprise that I'm part French. Or that I'd been to Paris before and the opulence mixed with the superficial charms felt like home.

We'd been so busy making travel plans and taking care of the kids there hadn't been any time left to work on our marriage. There never was. Even reluctantly letting Craig hold my hand while strolling through Montmart was out of the question. Four kids with eight hands ensured there was nothing left for Craig or I. There never was. God knew if we held hands it might lead to something more. And where the hell would we do that? The hotel bathtub?

The enchantment of Paris was part of our history. We'd first walked the streets when Craig's parents moved there with his two younger brothers in 1990 when his dad was commissioned to work on EuroDisney. Craig chose to stay in the States, finish college and prep for medical school. We were already engaged. Our wedding planned for two years from then, the month after I would graduate from college. I urged him to move and experience France for a year and a half but he decided to stay in the States. To be closer to me, even though he lived in Florida and I lived in New York.

We rendezvoused in Paris twice to visit his parents, make wedding plans and languidly stroll the streets. Amidst his two brothers who already lived there, two additional brothers visiting from Florida, his parents and some family friends who showed up unannounced and who Craig's parents were later forced to evict. Except for all that, it was totally passionate.

Two decades later, we were tour guides for the four elements. Who wanted to see the Mona Lisa at the Louvre. What we didn't know, even though Craig and I had been to Paris twice more after we'd gotten married, was that the Louvre was also home to the largest collection of Egyptian antiquities ever stolen by a Colonial empire. Take that, Egypt!

We were too damn tired to save money, so why not take the elevator to the top of the Eiffel Tower? It was money well spent because it was one of Jade's favorite memories. Since Craig and I were familiar with the city, we did our best to give the kids riveting cultural walking tours of the highlights. But the elements were content collecting and fighting over used metro tickets and feeding the pigeons outside Notre Dame. Stuff we could have done at home with elaborate homemade backdrops cut out of cardboard while saving thousands of Euros. Although it hardly seemed like money at all because the bills were blue, green and pink. It was Monopoly money. Until the bill collectors came.

When we returned from Paris, only three more weeks remained with Kim and family before they moved back to Colorado. In six months, we'd bridged the gap. The massive self doubt and veneer of perfection I'd tried to maintain that had sometimes held me back from developing authentic friendships in the past. Less than a year in, I was losing my partner in crime. Just when debauchery had become my favorite survival strategy.

We said goodbye in our typical fashion. She ding-dong-ditched my house and left a light-up, musical belly dance doll bought in the medina. Then she was gone.

~

A trek through the desert in December didn't sound Christmasy at all. Christmas was snow, hot cocoa, pork and cookies shaped like the michelin man. Wait a minute. Unless it was about Jesus, who'd been born in the desert. Wise men. Camels. Right, OK, so this was the perfect time to go to the desert. It would be a vintage, retro, back-to-basics Christmas. I couldn't have planned it any better. Except I hadn't planned it; our friends the Copseys had. Good thing, 'cause I would've totally screwed it up.

The Sahara Dessert is in the Southeast corner of Morocco and drifts into Algeria. It will be our longest road trip with the elements and the roads were twisty, turny and barfalicious. We required drugs. Dramamine and Benadryl for the kids. Wine for the adults. Since Jesus wouldn't be there to turn water into wine, we'd come packing. We needed to because we weren't staying at an inn, we were roughing it, camping in Berber tents on the dunes.

The change of scenery was dramatic. Leaving the lush greenery of Rabat, we traveled through the amber dirt movie studio town of Ouarzazate and continued past the palm-encircled oasis of Zagora until we reached the desert. Not that the elements noticed any of that because they were completely engrossed in their road companions, the four Copsey children. When the three-day journey finally ended, we found ourselves surrounded by dunes like a scene out of *The English Patient.* Except that was filmed in Tunisa.

Our camels were adorable in a gawkish, Lyle Lovett kinda way. River's camel belted out a protest even though he was the lightest haul of all. Camels tended to be temperamental, just like River. Their frothy mouths made them look rabid and there was a reason why they were banished to the desert...because camel farts are putrid. And that hump? It was conducive to a condition known as Camel Crotch. You could try to treat it with hydrocortisone cream but that just made the blowing sand stick to the infected area and increased the frictiony sandpaper effect. So, it was better to just ride it out. All part of the rustic, vintage Christmas experience.

The desert seemed like the best place to avoid the commercialism and consumerism Christmas had become. Just because there's no TV didn't mean there was no commercialism. It only meant entrepreneurs had to think outside the box and find the right spokesperson to promote their products. Thus dune kids. They appeared from nowhere while we jumped off and rolled down the barren dunes. They brought a bag filled with camels made of string. The boys were all of two and four years old roaming the desert by themselves. I'm sure their mom kicked them out of their tent by saying, "Stop fighting with your brother! Go outside and sell some camels we made from that unraveled camel hair sweater grandma knitted that you grew out of last year!"

The oldest removed the camels from the cloth bag and placed them in a long caravan in the sand in the slowest product display I'd ever witnessed. After all, what the hell was the rush? He probably had to milk a goat afterward; might as well milk the string camels. It was easier. They were extremely, silently persistent. The little one's eyes squinted a hole through my soul. Damn, they were good. I gave them all the money from my pockets and left them the toy camels. Maybe they'd get some time to play with them after milking the goats.

It was Sky's birthday. He'd outgrown any toy that didn't shoot something at really high speeds into something else and make it explode. Preferably Ember. That year there was no gift because we left it at home so it wouldn't get sandblasted. No cake because where the hell were we going to get one? So we stuck a single candle into a piece of Moroccan bread over lunch, sang *Happy Birthday* and rode camels. The most basic yet exotic birthday party ever. He probably wished we were back in America considering that Moroccan bread but he would never forget where he was when he turned twelve. I'll never forget he complained he couldn't go paint balling on his birthday.

## O CHRISTMAS TREE

**After Thanksgiving, Christians everywhere went on a quest for a Christmas tree. Maybe it would be a real tree or maybe it would be**

the one up in the attic covered in dust in need of fluffing and preening. Our family tradition in Colorado was to pay ten dollars for a permit to cut down a tree from Pike's National Forest, bundle up and trudge through the forest to find just the right one then slowly murder it with a hacksaw.

At first, I carried so much guilt about the whole murdering a real tree thing. That I was singlehandedly obliterating the world's forests by cutting one down. Turns out this was good for the densely populated timberlands and helped it to stay healthy. Guess I couldn't see the forest for the trees. Why did we dress up a tree like a Las Vegas show girl for a month to celebrate Jesus' birthday, anyway? Where in the world had this bizarre tradition started?

In a Muslim country, there weren't any real Christmas tree forest for us to save. What in the world were we going to do about a tree? Would it still be Christmas without one? What about gifts? Personally, I thought we should string some lights on the huge palm tree in the front yard. Except for one a fatal flaw—winter was the rainy season. Rain + electricity + tree + 4 kids = fatality. So I was talking to a friend when she mentioned she'd found trees and wrapping paper at a local store. We were so there!

That marked the first time in our family history we searched for a Christmas tree with a shopping cart. The elements wore shorts and listened to Arabic muzak playing overhead at the Marjane; also a first. It wasn't possible to have less Christmas spirit than we did right at that moment. We headed to the back corner where the store had a small Christmas section with garlands, Santa hats, candles and some trees. That's when we saw it. All one foot of it wrapped in cellophane for the dirham equivalent of $2. Our Charlie Brown Christmas tree. How would we select that one lucky ornament to decorate it? And where would we put it?

The upside of having a one foot tree was that it was portable. Sure, we could put it in the middle of the train set like Christmas tradition dictates. But why? If I was cooking and felt a little lonely, I could bring it into the kitchen with me. If the girls wanted to have a sleepover with the tree in their room, why not? It could be a centerpiece on the dining room table. Why bring a book to the bathroom when we could bring the Christmas tree? We could even take it on a road trip. Santa could build a pyramid of presents and put the tree on top like a star! And think how useful a little tree would be to construct a trap for leprechauns come St. Patrick's Day!

I was starting to think we'd been given a gift, the ability to think outside the box. It wasn't about a tree or whether it was real or fake. Or even if we had one at all. It wasn't about scoring wrapping paper. Or listening to the Little Drummer Boy with the incessant drumming that would drive us to overindulge in eggnog. It was about having the Christmas spirit regardless of where we were and what we had or didn't have. Now I wonder if I can buy some spirit at Marjane?

Oh, never mind all that crap. I just found a four-foot fake tree on sale at Label Vie!

# Chapter 8

# Talkin' 'Bout a Revolution

Spring had sprung in Africa...Arab Spring. Right before that, there was trouble in Niger. Al-Qaida claimed responsibility for two French citizens who'd been kidnapped and murdered. Within twenty-four hours, ninety-eight Peace Corps volunteers had been evacuated. Leaving their villages, projects, friends and pets in Niger to head for Morocco, a safe haven. The volunteers had two choices: a free ticket home to the States with a certificate saying that they'd completed their obligation, or await reassignment to a new, safer bug-infested country. Most of them couldn't get enough parasites, diarrhea, poverty and evacuations the first go-around and chose to do it all over again somewhere new.

Meanwhile, in Tunisia, peaceful demonstrations about unemployment and corruption suddenly turned violent. Tanks lined the streets, bullets flew and fires were set. While the president of Tunisia fled to Saudi Arabia, there wasn't a mandatory evacuation of Americans. But U.S. embassy families were offered the option to be evacuated to Morocco while things quieted down or until evacuations were mandatory. Many families stayed. Americans liked to exercise their right to tenacity and stupidity.

We were in the midst our own revolution at home. A teenager in training, Sky wanted more independence and his friends became increasingly important. I felt threatened that I wouldn't be relevant in his world much longer and fought to stay connected, even if I had to feign disinterest to do it. I had one powerful weapon I could always count on to rally the troops and get them on my side—food.

Sky was the only element with parent-teacher conferences and a half day of school. I'd had this date on my calendar for a week. I would pick him up from school and we'd have lunch together, go to his conferences, come back and cook authentic Moroccan couscous. We would talk, we would laugh, and we would enjoy each other's company without three other distractions. It would be the perfect day. Then again, I was prone to fantasy. I waited at the school for the bell to ring when I ran into the mom of one of Sky's friends.

"Can Sky come over and hang out with Nicholas today?" she asked.

Note: It was no longer a playdate because boys that age didn't play together anymore. They did things they could do alone together. Watching YouTube videos, for example.

"No, I'm sorry." I lied. 'Cause I was totally not sorry. "Sky and I have a playdate. I mean, a date. We're making couscous together." Step off, bitch!

"Oh, that's so nice!"

"Shh. Here he comes. Please don't mention you invited him over. 'Cause he'd definitely choose Nicolas over me."

Sky's approach was ambivalent and he avoided any direct eye contact with me.

"Hi! How was your day?" I asked.

"Good," he replied.

"Pretty sweet. It was a short day and now you're done and have a long weekend, huh?" Did young kids still use the word sweet or was that too archaic and old school?

"I guess."

I reviewed the unwritten middle-school mom rules. First, do not call him honey or any other affectionate term that indicated we were related and genuinely liked each other. Absolutely do not hug or wrap an arm around said child. Third, kissing your mom? In public? Are you kidding me? That would have been the kiss of death for his social life.

"So, I'm going to eat at the cafeteria with my friends. I'll find you later," he said.

"Ah, OK." I pretended that hadn't stung.

"I have some reading to catch up on anyway, honey." Oops. "Bud." I thought Bud was familiar enough without being too familiar. I could have been his cousin three times removed. Unless I was just super casually disinterested, like I'd forgotten his name or something.

After lunch, we went to his conferences. It had been especially hard for him to start middle school in a foreign country finding his way in a new culture, a new school, making new friends and constantly defending his American culture.

Sky had a unique brilliance about him. Even though he drove me out of my mind with it. I couldn't claim to understand him but I was overwhelmingly proud of the young man he'd become. And I started thinking about the day Craig and I chose him from all the boys in the orphanage and the director met our choice with disdain. She told us he'd never be able to learn English, much less amount to anything. If he hadn't been adopted, eventually he would have been sent to fight the war in Chechnya because he wouldn't have had a family to miss him. His alternative fate snuck up on me at the most inappropriate times. Tears of pride welled in my eyes mid-conference. Unwritten middle school rule number four: Do not cry at your child's parent-teacher conference.

~

"Can you get the carrots out of the fridge, honey?" I asked.

Once we were home alone, I was free to use terms of endearment. I pulled out the stock pot, the steamer and all the ingredients. Sky chopped the carrots, turnips, cucumbers and cabbage while I browned the chicken with olive oil, saffron, cumin, coriander and cinnamon.

When all the veggies had been prepped and the chicken golden, we placed the veggies on top in the stockpot, added the chicken stock and waited for it to boil. The real stuff happened in the kitchen. The jokes, the quips, and ultimately stories and questions both big and small. That was my invitation to his expanding universe that became more crowded every year with more friends, more challenges, more choices, more independence and more opportunities.

The pot boiled. Time to prepare the couscous. Sky massaged it with olive oil and butter then added salt and pepper. When it grew sticky, we put it in the colander on top of the boiling stockpot, turned down the gas, and allowed it to simmer and steam.

How had he reached twelve so quickly? Why won't he stop reminding me that in only three years he can get a driver's permit? Why did he always ask to wear deodorant but constantly forgot to wash his feet? When would he remember that his sleeve was neither a napkin nor a tissue? I was positive he knew the location of the hamper, so why were his clothes constantly on the floor? I had him for six more years. Thank god, because no one wanted to live with someone who forgot to put the milk away. I still had to teach him that. And so many other things.

The chicken and veggies were cooked through. The couscous wasn't done. It looked really easy to watch a Moroccan make it. My American ingenuity said we would finish the couscous over a smaller pot filled with boiling water. Then I burned it. Whoops. The kitchen filled with a non-authentic burnt semolina smell that lingered for days afterward.

Sky suggested we eat Moroccan style by piling the couscous, chicken and veggies into one big shared platter. Which must have meant I wasn't too gross or repulsive to share the same plate with him. The meal wasn't perfect, it wasn't even good but that didn't matter. It was couscous Friday and the whole family was home sharing the world's crappiest couscous.

~

Around that time my blog took off. People I wasn't even related to who didn't have any obligatory interest in my life were reading it now. Suddenly I was showered with compliments from strangers. None of which I took to heart because I was skeptical of their motivation. It triggered old insecurities and made me contemplate what they wanted from me. Most of the time I assumed it was a follow back on their blog. My assumption was that I was in blog debt to cyber interlopers and could only repay it by visiting their blog and complementing them in return. Which I refused to do under such oppressive, obligatory circumstances. So I didn't. Because I wasn't a flowery, coddling bullshit artist with the elements, I wasn't about to take on that role for someone I didn't know and who hadn't earned my trust. I'd been screwed that way before.

The thing with people who instantly love you is that at any second they can instantly hate you. So, in addition to receiving fan mail, I also started getting hate mail. To a few I'd become that foreign, overly critical of Morocco bitch. I thought I would hate hate mail. To my complete and utter shock, I didn't. In the process of revealing myself and my innermost thoughts to anyone in the world with a computer, I'd let myself become vulnerable. Somehow that vulnerability had thickened my skin and slowly turned into strength.

I didn't write to please the reader. I wasn't getting paid to write, so I didn't have any obligations to a boss, a brand or sponsors. For the first time in my life, the only person I wanted to please was me. That was the hardest job because I wasn't easy to please, in fact, I was an uncompromising, taskmaster bitch of a boss. But I was writing things I felt proud of, in an unobtrusive way, on the internet. If someone didn't like it, they could simply unsubscribe, unfollow or delete me. I had bigger concerns.

Like how my writing affected my family. I guess it was only a matter of time before Sky's friends found my blog. He was mortified I'd written about him. The vast majority of my posts were about me. But every once I wrote about the elements…only after a long session of grappling with whether it was necessary or whether it would be detrimental to them in any way. Having a writer in their life, especially when it was their mother, meant not living in anonymity because our lives were intertwined. We affected one another, we changed each other, we were part of the same story despite how much we sometimes wanted to deny it. Like after Sky's friends read the following post.

## THE OTHER MAN

As some of my closest friends know, I have another man in my life. I see him a couple times a week. Jade met him a few weeks ago and told me she thinks he's cute too. It's true. He doesn't speak English and I don't speak Arabic or French but that doesn't matter. We speak the language of love.

Barack (that's his name) is my favorite parking guy. If you don't live in Morocco, you might think it's weird to have a parking guy let alone a favorite parking guy. But if you live in Morocco, you've already pictured your own favorite parking guy and probably got the comforting smell of exhaust fumes accompanied by the urgent need to scrounge up some coins for his tip.

My guy works the parking lot of my favorite grocery store. I don't want to even tell you which one. Because, I admit it, I'm possessive and I don't want to share him. Oh, I know he has other clients but I like to think I'm his favorite. Not because I have an overinflated ego but because I overtip him. That's why I'm pretty damn sure he'd forsake all others for me. At least in my presence.

The first time I met him, he spotted me coming out of the store struggling to push my crappy unyielding Moroccan grocery cart. He gently took it from my hands so he could push it to my car. How's that for chivalry? How did he know which car was mine, you ask? First, it's a minivan. Second, it has a yellow diplomatic license plate. Third, she's a battered woman who earned the title Battlecar Gallactica and the instant recognition that goes with it.

Barack loaded up my junker and it seemed to me he'd performed more than 2 dirhams (the equivalent of less than 20 cents USD) worth of work so, I give him 10 dirhams. A love story had begun. I always looked for him in that cramped little parking lot and he always looked for my 10 dirham. I mean me. At least I thought so.

A couple of weeks ago I was driving through a street in Agdal by the French school. I saw her in her car acting all meek like she didn't know if she could back up more or not. And there he was. Barack. Working another street in a different part of town and directing her Citroen into a tight spot. Yeah, it's all sporty, new and unblemished. That bitch! Oh god, I bet she had it washed just to make it all nice and shiny for him too.

I didn't go see him for nearly two weeks after that. OK, so I was out of town for most of that. Still, no matter. I'm sure he felt my distant rage. I bet forgoing that $1.50 (depending on the exchange rate) a week really hurt. He's learned his lesson. I could totally see the remorse in his eyes when he loaded up my groceries this morning. Right before I caught him ogling that beautiful Mercedes I was parked next to.

# Chapter 9

## Seeds of Change

I'm a serial killer. I can't help myself. I've tried to stop. Yet whenever the opportunity presents itself, I'm there with my trowel and hoe. No plant is safe in my path. I must confess I also unintentionally murdered the first-grade tadpoles and roasted our guinea pig in the sun. That was just karma though because that guinea pig was evil. Not that that justifies anything. I do feel horrible guilt and remorse. So why, oh why, would I devise a plot to kill again?

Reasons 1, 2 and 3 are romaine, spinach and arugula. Lettuce was available at the supermarche (supermarket) but it was wilty, caked with dirt and laced with bugs. Another option was perfectly crispy romaine from the veggie dealer at the souk. The catch was he was the only guy in town with the goods and he knew it. He also knew exactly how much he could overcharge a skinny white chick looking for her salad fix.

We didn't know a damn thing about gardening. When was planting season? Would our garden plot get enough sun? Enough rain? The biggest question was, would I kill again? After consulting the internet, I was even more confused. I called my sister Kathy in Utah for a long-distance garden consultation.

"What the hell do I do with these seeds?" I asked.

"Don't worry," she said. "Just stick them in the ground. They'll grow."

"But when do I do this sticking them in the ground stuff?"

"You said there's no frost there and it's sunny with some rain. So, now."

"That sounds too easy."

"Marie, gardening is really easy."

"So easy even I can't screw it up? 'Cause, you know, I can screw anything up."

Turned out she was right. All that time I've been way over complicating things. All I needed to do was throw some damn seeds in the dirt. Maybe that was the problem with my marriage. I just needed to let the seeds that had already been planted ride out the frost, expose it to some sun and rain then simply let it bloom.

Egypt threw some seeds of its own around. The seeds of change began germinating when Mubarak was overthrown. No. That couldn't be happening. Not just two weeks after I bought six super cheap, nonrefundable tickets to Cairo. Again. Because I have impeccable timing like that.

Ever since our extensive tour and staycation at the Cairo airport, we'd been planning our return trip. Egypt might have won the battle but I was determined to win the war. Not that we'd figured out how to get those special visas we needed to enter the country. It wasn't for lack of trying. Craig called the Egyptian Embassy, we'd gone there in person, and we'd had locals call for us to sweet talk them in French and Arabic, to no avail. Obviously they've been too busy gossiping about Mubarak behind his back and planning a coup at the water cooler to get any real work done.

Getting visas wasn't our biggest problem. The U.S. Embassy personnel in Cairo were evacuated and a travel warning was issued. Americans weren't supposed to travel to Egypt. At that point, we've paid for *twelve* fucking nonrefundable tickets to Egypt. I didn't know how we were gonna get there and I didn't care anymore. We were going to Egypt, god dammit! We'd circumvent our own embassy to do it. Which was harder than it sounded when we knew every American who worked there socially.

We lived in a bubble. A bubble of privilege, crazy driving, parties, calls to prayer, travel, house help and parties. Did I mention parties? That was expat life inside the U.S. Embassy bubble in Morocco. We worked together, played together, went to school together, exercised together, traveled together and of course partied together. There was no escaping the bubbliciousness of it all.

The bubble was way weird. Whenever a diverse bunch of highly educated people with different politics, religion, temperaments, backgrounds, experiences, Northerners and Southerners were mixed, legions of spirited discussions resulted. Then put that group in a Muslim country, add children and little in the way of the comforts of home, and you get what amounts to a private New England boarding school. Not that I've been to one; I'm just guessing. Add more children, because the bubble encourages children. Then confine those people to a soapy, impenetrable invisible fence and that was life on the Embassy circuit.

We deluded ourselves for a long time that since Craig didn't work at the embassy, we weren't in the bubble. That was a huge misnomer. We didn't have to work at the embassy to be bubbly. Hell, we didn't even have to be American. All we had to do was hang out with a couple of Americans who were. Speaking English was essential though because it was imperative to know when people were talking about you behind your back.

Without having to say a word, the bubble knew things. Things like who you voted for in the last election, your SAT scores, where you were and who you were with Saturday night, the name of your childhood cat, if you're the one who hoards all the cheddar cheese in town, and whether you deuced at your child's birth. The bubble knew everything. Yet we still didn't have any idea what anyone at the Embassy really did. Because no one did what they claimed.

I denied my bubbliciousness for a long time. After all, I didn't work, I didn't like to talk, I didn't like bullshit, and I didn't talk politics or religion socially. I thought that made me super unimportant and uninteresting to the bubble. Later, I discovered otherwise. Right then, I thought I was on the edge of the bubble. But spheres don't have edges. They're filled with hot air that sooner or later gets blown right up your ass.

## TONY BENNETT

I love Tony Bennett! So who am I to pass up on an invitation to go to his house for lunch?

OK, you caught me. I'm talking about the U.S. Ambassador to Morocco, who bears a striking resemblance to Tony Bennett. I further confess I didn't have lunch with just him but a reception with him and about fifty other people. It was at his house though.

So, I was talking to my sister on the phone this week. We talk about all the familial stuff when she asks me what I'm up to. "We got an invite to the ambassador's house for this Fiftieth Anniversary of the Peace Corps thing-y," I said.

"What?" She was excited.

"I don't think I'm gonna go." Because I hate going to social functions trying to make small talk with people I don't know. Which is far better than making chitchat with people I do know but don't like. Since Craig has to go anyway and my sister thinks I should, I decide to brave it.

I dust off the one business casual day dress I own and a pair of high heels. Because this now ranks as one of those biannual events when I wear desperately grievous footwear. I pick up Craig from work and we head to the Ambassador's residence. I smooth down my dress and pick the panty wedgie out of my ass before we go in. Because I want to feel my best before going into a totally uncomfortable social function.

The ambassador greets us. This is my moment to say something really profound. Of course, that's not what happened.

"Has anyone ever told you you look like Tony Bennett?" I asked.

Apparently he's heard this before because he says, "I'm taller than Tony Bennett." Bitterly.

Note to self: Google how tall Tony Bennett is.

This uncanny ability to say just the wrong thing happens with more frequency than I'd like to admit. I'm gonna stick to a few polite hellos while I'm bee-lining to the buffet to stuff food in my mouth to keep it occupied. The place is swarming with the Peace Corps volunteers in town to celebrate the fiftieth year of do-gooding. So there might not be much food left. I don't think it's coincidence that all the male volunteers are wearing cargo pants or that their numerous pockets are bulging.

Unlike trying to make polite, intelligent but inoffensive conversation with diplomats, talking to the volunteers is always fun. I can say anything and they don't care if it's stupid or not. As long as it's in English. They're not listening anyway. They're casing the buffet for what will fit in their pockets without oozing and they're checking out other volunteers for that night's booty call. After drinking some iced tea and nibbling, the inevitable happens.

"Excuse me for a moment," I say semi-urgently. Which sounds a little more dignified than *Holy crap, I need to take a dump!*

It's hard to walk elegantly in high heels while clenching my butt cheeks. I find the restroom in the nick of time. As thoughtful as the design of the ambassador's home is, one would think air freshener would be in the bathroom. Because after I completely defile it, I would like to extend a little courtesy and attempt to leave no trace of my unmentionable deed. I know there's a budget crisis and all but sometimes spending a little money yields big rewards. A scented candle would be about $7, a can of air freshener about $4 and a book of matches $1. I'll bet the ambassador receives plenty of foreign dignitaries. Goodwill and world peace starts with leaving the powder room for the Ambassador of Syria powder fresh. It's worth a shot, isn't it?

As I begin my return to the reception, the speeches had already started. I'm trapped. I can't get out through the main entryway so I sneak through the kitchen for a stealth reentry from the side. That way I won't disrupt the quiet din of boring speeches no one gives a crap about anyway. Unfortunately I'm wearing heels I can barely walk in, or rather, they're wearing me.

I do my very best delicate Pink Panther sneak walk back from the shitter on my heels. Hushed audience. *Clomp, clomp, clomp.* Everyone looks in the direction of the noise, clumsy me. Now they all know where I was and what I did. Hopefully they can't smell it in the moist, humid Moroccan air. It's only a matter of time before someone else goes in there and figures out who violated the international peace agreement. And I want to be home in my flip flops and jeans laughing my ass off when they do.

# Chapter 10

## Being the Beckhams

Déjà vu. We presented our official passports with our official visas we jumped through so many hoops to get at Egyptian customs.

"I'll pretend I didn't see that," the officer says.

Apparently when personnel at a U.S. Embassy are evacuated, you can't travel on an official passport to that country. Oops. He points at the visa office in the hallway where we can get a regular tourist visa. Luckily, Craig in all his meticulous planning had insisted we get regular tourist passports before we'd left. Which was a huge pain in the ass in Morocco, just like everything else.

When we got them in the mail a couple of days before we left, we noticed their screw up. River was a female on his passport. It might have been because of his long hair, delicate features, and the fact that he'd always been quite pretty. We took it just in case because we didn't have time to amend it even though he was mortified. One passport sex change and one hundred dollars later, we were in Cairo looking at the outside of the terminal.

Cairo was one of the biggest and fastest growing cities in the world with a population of 20 million, the population of the top five most-populated U.S. cities combined. There was no hiding its enormity. That was evident in the congested traffic, the immense crowds, and the filthy streets littered with garbage. People were everywhere and they looked very similar to Moroccans except the women. In Egypt, far more women wore headscarves and burkas than in Morocco. I'd never not seen so many faceless women before. Which only made me watch more intently in search of clues about the lives lived by the women underneath. I wanted to know who would choose that life for them and how the revolution would change their future. Both being too complicated and irresolute to provide the conclusive answer I was looking for.

Even though the city was enormous and festooned with centuries-old Islamist architecture, our presence wasn't dwarfed. Being tourists at a time when there weren't tourists made us a spectacle. Revolution wasn't exactly good for tourism. Everyone noticed us, everyone had something to say to us, something to sell us, and everyone stared at us. They were happy we were there and thanked us for coming. I felt completely embraced by the Egyptians. Even if they were embracing me while sticking their hands in my back pocket for some baksheesh.

*n. pl. baksheesh: A gratuity, tip or bribe paid to expedite service, especially in some Near Eastern countries.*

While the U.S. government proclaimed Egypt unsafe for travel, I perceived us being overwhelmingly safe. I was prepared for pick-pockets, looting and chaos but that's not what we found. When we went to the ATM, it was guarded by a guy with a body shield next to a tank sporting a machine gun. I'd never been more sure we weren't going to be mugged. Sprayed by machine gun fire or run over by an antique Soviet tank supplied by the Russians maybe. Mother Russia, the birth place of the elements. Sky and River thought pyramids and hieroglyphics were cool but a glimpse of their heritage and martial law topped even that.

We'd done so much work to get to Egypt we hadn't prepared an itinerary. Coincidentally, Sky was studying Egypt in school so surprise! Pop-quiz fieldtrip! We let him figure it out and started in Tahir Square, the heart of the revolution. It was the third that had taken place there, preceded by the revolutions of 1919 and 1952. Third time's a charm, right? As we get closer to our destination, the Museum of Egyptian Antiquities, just off the square we spotted the burned remnants of the Ministry of Internal Affairs. Burned down March 22, a mere five days before our arrival. Of course, we hadn't known about that.

The museum was crowded with piles of unlabeled artifacts like a prodigious unorganized garage sale. It had been looted weeks before, which was unfathomable. How could more stuff have possibly fit in there? It was like *Hoarding: Buried Alive,* the Egypt edition. Plus most everything was enormous and made of stone. How could you steal a granite statue that weighed over a ton? You couldn't shove that into a purse. Which was exactly why I laughed when security checked my bag as we exited the museum.

Revolution graffiti was everywhere and so were post revolution t-shirts sold by opportunists with very few opportunities to sell them post revolution. I guessed they weren't made out of quality Egyptian cotton, either. So, if I did buy one, that shit was gonna shrink and bleed all over the rest of the laundry in what would be forever referred to as The Bloody Non-Egyptian Cotton T-shirt Revolution of 2011. Just as soon as we got one salesman to leave, another one approached.

Even though I wasn't going to buy one, I found it really hard to say no. That was, until I was approached by grown men leering at nine-year-old Jade. "How many camels for your daughter?" they asked.

Yeah, plural, because there was more than one.

"No! I will take your dirty mind along with the rest of you and shove your head up the ass of a camel. Don't think I can? Try me, dirty old man!"

Spring in Egypt marked the end of tourist season, or what would have been tourist season if the nation hadn't been selfish enough to revolt against an oppressive dictator. No place was more frequented by tourists and scam artists in Egypt than The Great Pyramid of Khufu. That day, it was just us against throngs of scam artists in waiting. We bypassed the fake park guide who charged for an unnecessary and fraudulent second ticket, we evaded the guys selling camel rides because we'd already done that in Morocco, and we shook off the vendors. The entrance to the pyramid was a welcome refuge.

Normally the narrow passageway up to the chamber would have been packed with tourists hunched over from the low ceiling trudging up the steep incline asphyxiating on the centuries-old stifled air. It was eerily vacant except for us. At the top, the King's chamber was completely empty 'cause the French stole all the crap and we already saw their proud display of Imperialist rape at the Louvre. When we returned, we met a guard.

"Psst. You want to see Queen's chamber?" he asked.

His eyes shifted between the entrance where the other guards were and us. That wasn't on the tour, it was dangerous, there was a chance we could get caught and something bad could happen. Hell, yeah!

We threatened the elements to be absolutely quiet with our eyes. They knew the look well. Then we scampered down the stairs to the basement, the proper place for a woman apparently. A seemingly interminable tunnel descended to the bowels of the pyramid. So maybe we weren't being good role models of integrity for the elements. Or maybe it was charitable giving so he could feed his family. It depended on how you looked at it. Which was exactly what morally reprehensible people said. We heard footsteps approaching, scurried up the stairs and baksheeshed him. The first time was always the hardest.

The second time we compromised our morals was at Al-Azhar Mosque, one of the world's oldest universities. It was definitely easier now that we'd become baksheesh whores. That was one of the few mosques that allowed non-Muslims inside as long as women covered their hair with a loner headscarf supplied at the entrance. Chance of lice and/or scabies at no extra charge. A man approached.

"Psst. You want to go to top of minaret? View of whole city for twenty Egyptian pounds."

By that time, we knew the price was bullshit. It would be more than twenty pounds and we might see 20% of the city then pay more to see the whole thing or something like that. But we've already corrupted the elements morals. What's once more gonna hurt?

His friend guarding the door collected the money. We climbed the dark spiral staircase lit only by a sequence of matches burned down to the nub. When we emerged at the top, the day was golden with late afternoon sun for our rooftop panoramic view of the mosque, the university, and part of the ancient city. He offered to take a picture of the family, one of the few we would have all together because we didn't pass off our camera to strangers in Cairo. We didn't want to have to pay to get it back, if that would even be an option. We figured we outnumbered him and could take him if we need to.

"Something for me?" he asked.

Craig gave him something but it wasn't enough. It was never enough. He turned his pockets inside out to give him a visual. 'Cause Cairo sucked us dry and I couldn't wait to head south to Luxor. To escape the big city, the scams, and pollution so dense my boogers had turned black.

## FIVE STAR

Scanning the passengers on the plane, I assess that we're the only tourists on the flight from Cairo to Luxor. As the plane climbs, we stray from the path of the Nile and into the red lands. This inhospitable desert is void of any of the 20 million people who overcrowd the capital. Peering out from the airplane window, I only see ripples of dirt for miles. In an hour we will reduce the beleaguering populace by 19.5 million.

Unlike the practical apartment where we stayed in Cairo, in Luxor we'll be staying at a five-star hotel. This is huge. We are not five-star hotel stayers. We can't afford to be. But because of the deep we-have-no-guests-during-the-revolution discount, this posh hotel is now within our budget. It boasts three pools, a waterslide and a mini-zoo. Sky sees the plaque inside the lobby proudly displaying the stars and utters what we all know to be true.

"This is way above our class," he said.

Yes. It's true. We're more two-star kind of people. Which is precisely why I started in on them.

"See that plaque? It's a reminder to use your five-star behavior. Which means don't wrestle your brother, don't punch your sister. And for god's sake don't whine. We're in the Disney Land of Egypt, OK? It's the second-happiest place on earth. And don't cop any five-star attitudes! I'm watching you. This is the apex of your life. Don't know what that means? It means the rest is downhill from here. Especially if you don't behave. Oh and have fun. But not too much fun."

The next day we took the hotel shuttle bus into town. Our self-guided tour would start at Karnack Temple, the preeminent structure when this was Thebes before it was destroyed in 335 B.C. by that cocky jerk Alexander the Great. When we arrive, they're all waiting. Apparently the whole town knows the hotel shuttle bus schedule. Even if there are less people begging and hassling than in Cairo, if someone is always hassling you, it really doesn't matter how many there are. Craig makes a game out of the unwanted attention and the kids join in. I can't handle it though. Seeing all the need makes me melancholy and I retreat inward. I can't look at them, let alone talk to them. So I put on my oversized sunglasses to disappear because I feel so guilty and sullen. Now I'm the snooty, privileged, unsmiling Caucasian woman with a slew of cute kids. I've become Posh Spice.

The beautiful temple is surrounded by a cloudless sky. Although we could really use some cloud cover 'cause it's hot as hell. The kids are melting into a puddle. We're swimming in the Beckham kids' five-star attitudes. If we were the Beckhams we'd have a nanny to deal with the messy details. We'd probably have four. We need nannies! Where the hell are they? Unfortunately, five-star hotels don't come equipped with them. So, drenched in sweat and completely exhausted by noon, we head back to the hotel pool. It's hard being the Beckhams without their money, influence, or nannies.

The next morning we head to the Valley of the Kings where 62 pharaohs lie entombed and even more are waiting to be discovered. If yesterday was hot as hell, today it's actually hotter than hell. The sign says we can't take pictures and must relinquish our cameras to the guards. We know enough to know that leaving our cameras with the security guards isn't safe, so we hide them deep in our bags.

Little relief from the stifling heat is available except inside the dark sepulchers. We're at the last one open for touring, Merenptah's chamber. A guard gestures to us with his hands. He's speaking in Arabic but we know what he wants. So we follow him past the barricade. He leads us down under Merenptah's sarcophagus until we're all cowering. And we're touching the inside of a Pharaoh's ancient crypt. We hand him our camera and he snaps a picture just as we hear voices. We scramble back up and discreetly baksheesh him. I don't want to brag but we've become quite proficient in baksheesh.

That night we eat dinner outside with a view of the Nile. The elements sit at a table next to ours. Separate but equal. It's one of those rare moments where they've called some kind of truce and they're kind and polite to each other, even passing the salt. Unlike the hundred million other moments when you're sure one of them could end up dead and we'd have to spend our Saturdays visiting one in prison.

This is precisely when I started sobbing uncontrollably. Not because I was so happy the elements were being good but because there was a magnificent buffet and we couldn't eat it all. So many Egyptians would be going to bed hungry. And here we are in a five-star hotel surrounded by more food than we could eat in an entire year. It felt criminal. It was such a relief to cry, even though it didn't change anything. I should allow myself to do it more often.

We'd met Ashraf the day before. There was something different about him. He wasn't like the rest of the hagglers. He could sense our weariness. I'm guessing he's well-educated and there just aren't many jobs for professionals, or many jobs period. Evidence of Arab brain drain that helped spur Arab Spring. We took him as our official guide for the last day and a half. True to his word, he never pressured us or set a price. He simply asked that we pay him what we thought was fair. After he took us around the city that day, he told us we could take a sunset cruise up the Nile in his boat.

We arrived at the marina at precisely 4 p.m. Ashram was waiting with his son and led us right to his boat. How romantic is a sunset cruise? Especially when we're on a sailboat and there's no wind. Not a gust, not a breeze, not a draft, not a puff. We helped row upstream to Banana Island. It was a long slow crawl, so our cruise took longer than planned. Now it was pitch dark on the crocodile-infested Nile. At least we wouldn't see it coming. Plus, there was something far worse than crocodiles...mosquitos. Swarms of insidious mosquitos out for blood. We became their unwilling donors. Finally we reach the far bank and pay Ashram. While we can't feed all the starving Egyptians, we did feed one family for at least two weeks, maybe more.

The last day, we ventured into town one more time and spent the morning loading up on trinkets for the elements. We helped them bargain, except for Sky who had it down. He learned from Craig to pretend not to care if they come down to his price and to walk away to bait them to the chase. He's good. And now everyone's got a little something to remember Egypt by. Not that any of us could really forget it.

In a taxi on the way to the airport, hundreds of people with signs celebrated the success of the revolution. That's what we thought we saw, anyway. It wasn't until we got home we realized we'd actually seen the continued unrest. The week after we left, thousands of demonstrators barricaded themselves in Tahir Square demanding the removal of the military council. It turned violent and over seventy demonstrators were beaten. At least one was killed.

The thing about revolutions is that things always get worse before they get better.

# Chapter 11

## Natural Disasters

After our return, more uprisings rocked Libya and Syria while a tsunami hit Japan. The two events that hit closest to home were Osama Bin Laden's death and the bombing at the Argana Cafe in Marrakech. We'd eaten there many times, sometimes having dinner on the balcony overlooking Jamaa el-Fna square watching the tooth pullers and storytellers. More often we'd stop at the glacee counter where they scooped the most delicious fig and avocado ice cream in Morocco. The counter and surrounding facade were gone now. It blew straight off in the bombing that killed seventeen people.

As a parent, there's a constant struggle to ensure your kids feel safe in an increasingly unsafe world. I wanted the elements to live life head-on without fear. Do it all now because who knows about tomorrow? At the same time, I wanted them to be cautious so they would have a future. I didn't want to tell them the bitter truth that none of us was safe anywhere at any time. That the fallacy of safety was nothing more than a soothing blanket that suffocates and isolates if you don't come up for air.

My instinct was to swaddle them and protect them because they were my babies. I wanted to tell them delusional fairytales, that everything would be okay and we would all die of old age in our sleep, happy with the lives we'd led. Except fairytales were brutal. Somebody always died and someone was always evil. Just like in real life. Which was why I would rather take them to Disneyland in the middle of August, stand in 100-degree heat plus humidity listening to them whine while waiting for It's a Small World with that stupid hypnotizing song every day for a year rather than tell them the harsh realities of the world. Albeit delicately.

"Mom," Jade said, "I heard at school that ice cream place in Marrakech got bombed."

Oh crap! "Yeah, it did. Sad, huh? " I said.

"Yeah. Did anyone die?"

"Yes. Five Moroccans and twelve foreigners. Listen, there are some crazy hurtful people in the world. And even though this happened in a place you've been to, the chances of something like this ever happening to you are infinitesimal. Do you know what the means?"

"No."

"Like, really, really, really small. Bad things happen sometimes. The important thing is to always listen to that little voice inside you that tells you when things don't feel right. *Always* trust yourself." Spoken by someone who'd learned that lesson the hard way.

"Can we still get ice cream when we go to Marrakech?"

I'd thought I was teaching her a lesson. I'd tormented myself trying to present it gift-wrapped in just the right way when she taught me to just say it as simply and directly as possible. And assure her that no matter what happened, there would always be ice cream.

~

I wasn't supposed to be happy when our therapist Emma told us she was moving to New Zealand but I was. We'd been seeing her every week for months, and although I would miss the aroma of her soups simmering on the stove, I wouldn't miss her prying my feelings out of me. It was far easier to pretend I didn't have emotions than to figure out how to recognize and determine what to do with them.

But that's precisely what she helped me do. I'm not going to lie; I don't like acknowledging hurt, pain, frustration, disappointment, shame, needs and wants. I know I'm not the only one. While I never even knew they were there before, because I stuffed them so far down, now I can feel them and acknowledge them. Sometimes that's all I seem to need to work through them.

Then there were the other times when I needed to share my feelings with Craig. I'd always shrouded my thoughts in secrecy. Divulging them was excruciating even with him. He's always supportive and attentive but he doesn't bullshit either. He has a way of telling it like it is, logically without undo flattery. That's one of the things I love about him. He grounds the captive emotional chaos that surges in my head. I base all of my decisions on how I feel while Craig analyzes, plots, charts things on a graph then, after considering all the data, takes action. I simply get a good feeling and dive in headfirst. Or get a bad feeling and completely avoid the situation. Unless the good feeling turns bad, which means I fucking dive, crack my head open and almost bleed out while subversively avoiding anyone who could suture it up.

My relief that therapy was over came at the price of Craig's anxiety. He liked having someone to talk to. Someone who knew our whole story with whom he could commiserate about what a pain in the ass it is to live with someone who doesn't want to talk, hold your hand or depend on you. He worried that when therapy ended we would stop progressing or worse, back track. He didn't want our marriage to fall apart.

At that point, neither did I. Somehow, even though I'd fought therapy and had done the minimum needed to scrape by, my emotional narcolepsy had disappeared. I'm not a psychologist or anything but I'm gonna say that was probably both good and relevant. Maybe I learned what I needed to and it was time to move on…on our own. Unless I was merely lying to myself so I could avoid things like I always did.

Without all that to-ing and fro-ing to Emma's house, forced talking, trying to get in touch with my emotions, feeling like shit about myself for hours afterward and wondering why Craig hadn't figured out he deserved better, I had more time on my hands. In the past I'd always used to fill it by pushing people away from me. Deflection and self hatred were great time fillers and not to brag but I was really, really good at them. Gifted even. Unlike anything else in my life.

Or I was, until I totally messed up and let people get to know me. The real me. Not the perfect plastic version that was neither perfect nor a result of plastic surgery. I was sure there was no link between letting my guard down and therapy. Unless it was Emma's bergamot aromatherapy. In which case, I'll concede to that.

~

I met Faith at our kids' Saturday baseball games. I liked her immediately with her warm, welcoming, all-knowing Ally Sheedy eyes. She was a quiet introvert like me. So at first I thought, like I always do, she was talking to me every week out of pity. She was working on her degree in counseling, so it was easy for me to degrade myself into believing I was her community outreach practicum for awkward adults who lacked social skills.

My suspicions continued for months until we realized we were kindred spirits. Both of us shared self-deprecating thoughts. Our default setting was the assumption that we would be rejected, and that made us feel like we stood naked on stage in front of our whole graduating high school class wearing only that stupid hat with the tassel.

That's when we became The AntiSocial Social Club (ASS). We were a secret society and we weren't accepting applications. Except for Jenny who rounded out our trio. Unlike Faith and I, Jenny wasn't a bit antisocial; she was a giant extrovert. At 5' 10" tall, she was a giant by Moroccan standards. She had all these weird extroverted ideas too. She didn't think a party was really a party until she'd arrived. Unlike Faith and I who assumed we made the party list by mistake.

We didn't know how we'd become friends with someone so opposite and who held a completely different outlook on life. Then we realized it was the perfect parasitic relationship. Extroverts needed attention. As introverts, we needed to divert attention away from ourselves to someone who actually wanted it. Naturally, Jenny became the president of ASS. It didn't hurt that she knew French, worked at the Embassy, and knew all the bubble gossip. Plus, because she took time to chat with real live humans, she knew how to print a shipping label at the self-service post office using the ornery printer that never worked. While that might sound small, trust me, mail ranked just below food in importance to an expat. She knew people, she liked things orderly in a very OCD way, and most importantly, she could order our food for us in restaurants in her most hilarious American-tinged French accent.

~

I was still working out twice a week in Sara's fitness classes. I was definitely getting stronger; I could open the cumbersome bulletproof door to the embassy one-handed to reach the post office. Where I was also armed with the secret to printing a shipping label solo. Steal the blank adhesive label from the DPO, print it at home, and return with the package only to find the postal workers out to lunch. Or closed for Groundhog's Day.

I'd made a horrible first impression with Sara when we'd met so she'd pegged me for a slacker and a troublemaker. Which was partially true. After Kim left, I became a regular one-woman snark show at her fitness classes. Freely speaking the berating self-commentary I'd always kept secretly stashed away in my head. Surprisingly, verbalizing took the sting out of them. It was also a great social survival technique. I'd become a satirist, entertaining anyone who coerced me into conversation, but only at small intimate gatherings. I was never interested in the limelight. Instead, I learned to manipulate the beam to reflect it at those around me. At some point, I'd won Sara over and we became inseparable.

I still missed my girlfriends from Colorado. Before I'd left, my friend Kirsten had been in the process of a divorce. She returned to school so she could support herself and her kids, and I wasn't there to help with any of it. I felt guilty for having left when she'd needed me most. She'd been left in the very capable, nurturing hands of our other mutual friends, though. Lori had known Kirsten years before I'd met either of them. And if anyone could nurture the hell out of you while making you laugh with her quick sarcastic wit until you snorted or pissed your pants, it was Lori.

Then there was Judy, uber mom extraordinaire, known for carefully and thoughtfully overscheduling her life and that of her kids in an effort not to miss anything. Which frequently required that she flake when she realized she couldn't be in two or three places at once. Then came Suzanne, my most devoutly serious friend who always lent a devoutly serious ear to whatever ailed a friend. Last and definitely not least was Mary, my roller derby wife, aka Mama Beast. She looked all sweet and innocent but she could knock you on your ass without you knowing until it was much too late. When I was with her, I felt younger and hipper.

I would soon return to my Colorado girls and so time with my new girlfriends in Morocco passed quickly. My days were spent making jam out of the mystery fruit that grew on a tree in my yard with Sara. We discovered later that we hadn't made jam; we'd actually made delicious chunky preserves out of loquats.

Then I invited myself on a disastrous overnight trip to a spa with the ASS where everything was closed for construction, Faith went home ill, and Jenny and I ended up in the bathtub together. Making our own do-it-yourself spa spreading yogurt on our faces and scrubbing our feet with scouring pads. Sara and I went to a Cat Stevens concert at the Mawazine Festival with our husbands to discover that Moroccans didn't know the words to the songs that came after he converted to Islam either.

Soon after that, we scored boar meat through Claire who got it from some hunters who worked at the United Arab Emirates Embassy who couldn't eat pork. When it turned out to be too big to fit in my oven, we borrowed Faith's grill to barbecue it then totally pigged out at the exclusion of our Muslim friends. And our Mormon friends because I marinated that sucker in a whole bottle of red wine.

When I discovered tribal belly dance on the internet, I ordered a Rachel Brice instructional DVD and Sara came over to do it with me. When Sara googled up some pole dance videos, we tried to figure out how to get a pole to Morocco and install it in our houses. Sadly, it never transpired. We spent as much of our free time with our friends as possible. Unless it was spent traveling. Until we combined them and started traveling with our friends whenever our schedules and travel destinations allowed.

## ROAD TRIPPIN'

Moroccan road trip, Loerzel style!

School: Take the elements out for an unexcused absence (which excuse me, I think being the kids' parent is enough of an excuse). I had to sign three forms for each kid. Jade, who was learning her times tables, knew that was twelve freakin' forms. All of which declared that I was indeed the world's worst mother for allowing my kids to miss a day at their crap-ass school. In addition to acknowledging that now they would never get their first choice of colleges and would thus never amount to anything. And I couldn't sign papers claiming I was the worst parent because I firmly believed I was at least the second to worst. So forget the forms. The elements are comin' down with a fever. Road Trippin' Fever!

Cats: We need to find sitters for both our official cat Maddy and the unofficial outdoor stray cats we feed. Last time we left Maddy, she'd just had emergency surgery from a stray cat attack (which has since been deported from our neighborhood) and was on antibiotics that made her puke all over the sitter's apartment. This time the cat sitter will come to our house. What could possibly go wrong? At least she can puke in the comfort of her own home. Oh wait, that's my house. Dammit.

Tunes: We did not have a DVD player in the car so the music we brought on road trips was even more crucial to our survival. Pre-trip, I must rid the car of CDs I play while cruising around town sans kids. You know, the really good ones I jam to by myself at the top of my lungs with the f-bomb in them. Road trips require a kid-appropriate mix. But I can only listen to the overwhelmingly optimistic song Peace Train without wanting that train to crash so many times.

Oh, and the radio stations? They play a mix of Arabic music, frap (my abbreviation for French crap), and the worst American music that inevitability has expletives because they don't bleep that s#@* out here. And I f&*^%$#% hate that!

Cash: Most hotels, restaurants and vendors didn't take credit cards. Traveling as a family of six necessitated bringing a buttload of cash. And ATMs? Don't count on finding a working ATM if you travel in Morocco. Ever. It will inevitably be the day you need it that the machine isn't working. Because they frequently don't work, no one will know the reason and so no one will be able to fix it. Load up on cash like a Colombian drug lord. Carrying around wads of money makes you a bit paranoid. Kinda like a Colombian drug lord.

Coins: Coinage was completely different than cash in Morocco. Coins don't come out of the ATM machine that don't work. Yet so many things in Morocco required exact change. It was extremely hard not to use up coins as soon as we got them. It took a month of consciously stockpiling for a road trip. After all, we needed it for the bathroom attendants at every rest stop (with four kids, that's tons of coins), the parking attendant and the gas station attendant.

Yes, they only have full-service gas pumps in Morocco. It's exactly like America in the 1950's except totally different.

Snacks: What is worse than four whiny fighting kids who don't have a DVD player on a road trip? Four whiny fighting kids who don't have a DVD player on a road trip and are hungry. Pack plenty of snacks. 'Nuff said.

Earplugs: I cannot express how many times earplugs saved us from killing one or more of the elements on road trips. You think seat belts save lives? Earplugs save even more!

Wine: We didn't leave home without it. Enjoying a glass of wine with earplugs while munching on a snack of soy wasabi peanuts is the only way to travel when you have to travel with kids. It was as close as we were going to get to a childless vacation. Of course, if partaking in wine meant we'd made it to our destination without killing anyone, including pedestrians, we would need to toast to that. Maybe a few times.

Birth Control: Had I packed my birth control pills? As if the elements themselves weren't birth control enough. God knows I did not want to road trip with five kids! Not that there would be any activity that could possibly result in births that need controlling because again, we were traveling with four kids! Often times we all stayed in the same room. The real reason I made sure to have them? So I didn't have to pack tampons.

Medications: The chance that at least one kid would be sick on the trip? Pretty good. So we stocked our own pharmacy including enemas for the chronically constipated element who shall remain nameless. No one wanted to be woken up at 2 a.m. with a kid in pain from impacted poo. Moroccan pharmacies weren't open 24/7 like in the States. So we would have been shit out of luck.

Mosquito Repellent: Luckily we didn't live in the malarial zone. But what if we ran into that one mosquito that was on vacation from the Congo? Well, let's just say I'd rather be prepared for that by not being bitten in the first place.

Hopefully we had everything we might need. Who was I kidding? I forgot something major every trip. As long as we had the elements we could survive anything. Shots of Benadryl were just bonuses.

# Chapter 12

## SUMMERTIME

By the time we'd lived in Morocco fifteen months, I was knee deep in hate with the kids school. Overall, it was a complete disorganized mess. The nurse's office gave Jade cough medicine without our permission. Jade's teacher called the class losers and idiots then denied having done so to the administration even when other kids confirmed it was true. River and Sky were unfortunate enough to have the yeller for a teacher. Not that they haven't been yelled at before but that was my job. If I'd thought it was acceptable for them to be yelled at in school, I would homeschool them.

The school counselor was no use because she had married the yeller. Even though her kid was also in Jade's class and she could have asked her daughter what was going on, she blindly defended the teacher. Implying Jade was a liar. That's when Jade's teacher started sucking up to me with millions of compliments because she knew that I knew she was a big, fat liar.

Most parents I talked to didn't like the school either and most didn't do anything about it. In Colorado, I'd always supported my kids teachers. I volunteered, I planned the class parties, and was the room mom in my kids' classes. Morocco was completely different. I became "that" mom. The one who regularly called the school and sent e-mails to complain. It was a new and uncomfortable role, seeing as how I chronically avoided conflict at all costs.

Craig and I referred to the principal as Mr. McClueless because he was oblivious to what was going on in his own school. Including a bullying problem of epic proportions. The situation was so unnerving and unsafe we discussed returning to the States a year early. I informed the school of our concerns in writing but they didn't respond. They didn't care. They harvested a fresh crop of American diplomats' kids every year and the government flipped the bill for it. We were irrelevant and replaceable.

We were debating the pros and cons of leaving Morocco early when it happened. The unfortunate bullying incident couldn't be denied because it was posted on YouTube. After a long-overdue uproar from parents, the administration finally expelled the four responsible students which resulted in an even larger international rift at the school. The expelled students' parents took the matter to Moroccan court. Pending a settlement, the court determined the school needed to educate the ousted students. We waited anxiously for a couple of months. If the court didn't uphold the expulsion, we would pack our bags.

Thankfully, it did. Despite our distaste for the school, we decided to stick it out for another year. Which, coincidentally, would bring with it a new principal for the following academic year. Being in Northern Africa, traveling and watching history unfold was worth any hit the elements took academically.

Once our priorities were straight and our fate had been decided, we focused on being a family. Taking the elements to the medina to blow their allowance on laser pointers and trinkets. Listening to Car Talk on NPR's internet stream. Making ridiculous music videos to post on my blog. Riding Rabat's brand new tram line back and forth with nowhere in particular to go. Visiting the zoo from which we were sure the animals could easily escape if they wanted. But, they probably didn't want to because there really wasn't all that much to do in Rabat.

It was much the same during the dreaded summer break. Weird, because in the States summer was my favorite time of year. There was so much to do it was hard to cram it all in over just two short months. Not so in Morocco. There was no YMCA goat milking day camp or beach volleyball league. Rabat in summer was a virtual ghost town. Most diplomats on the embassy circuit moved to new posts in June and July. If they weren't slated to move to another exotic foreign destination just yet, they vacationed in one. With most of our English-speaking friends gone, the elements had only each other. And if you remember, they hated each other, so summer became one really, really long hate-fest. It sucked.

Craig did most of his travel for work over the summer. To remote African countries that are even more exotically barren of kid's entertainment than Morocco. At least he didn't have to take the elements. I, on the other hand, spent every day wracking my brain for anything that would fill a few minutes strung together. So we made Cheez-It crackers from scratch, weapons out of sticks and duct tape, and hunted cockroaches. The elements had a date war with the sweet fruit that dropped from the palm tree. By the way, it hurts like a bitch to get whipped by a goddamned date.

Before the Copseys left, we laid claim to their super ghetto 1970's trampoline with exposed metal springs and no safety net, which made it even more dangerous. As did a jumping date war. Going to the hospital would give us something to do. An educational summer fieldtrip. One that against all odds never happened. What did happen was that Ember, our fire child, burned two holes in it with a magnifying glass. She burned her name into the plastic seat of a bike the same way. Oh, and a huge hole in her sneaker. That's how boring summer was. Boring enough to sit still for more than twenty minutes at a time with a massive cramp in her arm from holding a magnifying glass at precisely the same trajectory until it smoldered. That was when we realized she was a pyro. Conversely, she learned it was better to burn her siblings' names in things.

The summer was about to get even worse. Our second Ramadan was fast approaching and we already knew enough to dread it. Thirty consecutive days of Muslims denying themselves food, water, tobacco, sex and alcohol. All that denial and self-discipline was supposed to teach patience, spirituality and humility. All I knew was that it wasn't fun to be around people who weren't eating, drinking, smoking, having sex or drinking. Edgy doesn't even begin to describe it.

## LIFE'S A BEACH

We went to have a good time. Of course, I had to convince Sky he actually wanted to go to the beach. Or that he was going to the beach whether he wanted to or not. I mean, it's the freakin' beach, for god's sake! Who doesn't want to go to the beach? The one we're going to is going to be too crowded, he said. I couldn't think of anything else to do and I'd already packed the lunch and the plan had been set in motion. So we're going, like it or not.

I asked the kids to pack the boogie boards, umbrella, and the bag with the towels and blanket that was on the kitchen counter. Again and again. Then Sky complained he didn't want "that" kind of sandwich, the kind I'd made. After he'd silently watched me make it and pack it. I wanted to whack him with that horrible, disgusting sandwich but it wouldn't have hurt enough and it wouldn't get us any closer to the beach. Instead, I checked to see that each child was wearing a bathing suit, which was a much more tedious process than I will detail here.

We're almost ready to head out the door when the phone rings. It was Craig calling from Cameron, so I had to take it. We talked for about five minutes while the kids loaded the car. Then we all piled in for the thirty minute drive to our favorite beach.

When we get on the coastal road, the traffic is heavier than usual. This is a bad sign. It's going to be packed. The Moroccans are cramming in their last beach outings before Ramadan. Sky was right. They'll be in the water boogie boarding anyway, I told myself, so it won't be a big deal to anyone but me who'll be sitting on the shore. We pull in and unload the car. I'm acting all glass-half-full so I don't throw the drink or just the glass at someone.

I'm making everyone carry their own boogie board. I'm so mean. Then I parcel out the umbrella, cooler, a couple of wetsuits and a chair. They're sure this is child slave labor. We haul our beach necessities across the busy road through the alley that smells like concentrated cat piss until we get to the congested beach, which smells like cat piss strewn with rusty cans and garbage. I busy myself organizing and setting everything up when Sky asks where the beach blanket is.

"I don't know, where is it? I only reminded you to pack it a mere five times!" I said.

Of course, the bag that the blanket was in also contained the towels.

After I'd finished talking with Craig, I'd forgotten to check that everything had been done. I don't know if I'm more pissed at myself, at him, or that everywhere in Morocco smells like cat piss. I'm definitely not pissed at me because I'm way too busy pitying myself. It's his fault and the fault of all the one-eyed, three-legged feral cats who probably drink puddles of piss in the alleyways then piss out super-concentrated piss. All I know is I'm not driving thirty minutes home to get anything.

OK, I can solve this. We'll simply go to one of the handful of beach stands and buy towels. I leave the boys to hold down the fort and take the girls with me. We had to park way down the road, so we endure a long backtrack to civilization and the vendors. It's still early and most of the stands aren't open yet. The two that are don't have any towels for sale. Not even one. I'm starting to feel panicky because I left the boys on the crowded beach in Morocco and I don't know how to say "towel" or "someone stole my boys and sold them to a leather tannery in Fez and I'm afraid I'll never see them again and if I do they'll permanently smell like wet leather" in either French or Arabic. Really? Why hadn't I packed the French phrase book for the beach? What was I thinking?

The girls and I make it back to our umbrella where the boys are waiting, thank god. But the elements are asking to go home. Oh, hell no. We're staying. I don't care how much it sucks, I haven't come all this way for nothing.

"I packed lunch, so we're eating it here," I command.

Everyone races to dig through the cooler to get their sandwiches. The worst sandwiches that have ever been packed for the worst day at the beach ever and they choke them down. Then they see the donut guy. Yes, every beach has a donut guy, a guy with a thermos of instant coffee, and a guy with a camel for rides up and down the beach.

I will do about anything to make this work at this point, so since they ate their sandwiches, I totally give in to buying them the donuts they're begging for. Although in Morocco they're called beignets, which is just French for greasy, sugar-sprinkled fried dough with a hole in it. Turns out eating a donut is only a good thigh killer and not a good time filler.

Ember started digging a hole. This is promising, 'cause we're working minute by minute now. Then they spot the toy vendor walking the beach selling balls made in China. Which leads my kids to ask why everything comes from China. Then one of them insists Canada is also in the top three exporters of products. Oh Canada? I'm as patriotic as the next person but I don't think so. I think you've mistaken Canada for Korea or something. (I googled when we got home. Surprisingly, Canada is actually number nine in worldwide exports while South Korea is number six, which makes me right, sort of.)

Anyway, the whole line of questioning on world trade did get me to buy a ball that looks like a watermelon that was probably made by a kid in China and was sold by a Moroccan kid with beignet sugar all over his face. At least I think that's what that was.

I finally sit down in the chair we schlepped here to relax but after only five minutes of a whirlwind game of dodge-a-toxic-Chinese-melon, the elements are done. Unequivocally. They all announce in unison that they voted and it was unanimous, they were ready to go home. Nothing in our house is ever unanimous. No one has ever used that word in a sentence before. They know exactly how to manipulate me while improving their SAT scores at the same time.

Our day at the beach lasted an hour. The car trip there and back took just as long. All that work only killed two hours of our long summer day. The remainder of it will be spent cleaning the copious amounts of sand out of our nooks and crannies. Life is definitely not a beach. Unless, unfortunately, it is!

# Chapter 13

## Self-medicating Sociopaths

By traveling, we managed to escape most of Ramadan before I wondered what I'd missed by having avoided it. Feeling really, really empty yet filled to the brim with spiritual enlightenment, perhaps? Maybe it was my childhood Catholic guilt lingering from that Ash Wednesday the teenaged me had tried to fast but didn't make it past 1 p.m. then gorged on jellybeans. In my defense, they were shaped like eggs, the international symbol of spring and rebirth, so it was in keeping with the spirit of the season.

Just to make sure my soul was in the clear, I would seek absolution through Muhammad. I was sure Jesus wouldn't mind. So, with a couple days of Ramadan left, I decided to fast for a whole day. Which was such American-express-drive-thru thinking, to condense thirty days of purification into twenty-four hours. To get the real authentic Ramadan experience, I'd have to take up smoking just so I would have to quit nicotine and food at the same time. That would be a far more credible Moroccan Ramadan experience since there are so many smokers here.

I made it the whole day without food and without any epiphanies. Unless my revelation was that I like food a whole lot. I wrote a post about my fast for the blog entitled "Quick, I Gotta Fast." While I thought it was a funny take on Catholicism, Islam, fasting, bake sales and American express thinking, one reader interpreted it as mocking Islam. I thought I'd been mocking myself, Catholicism and Islam in a holy trinity of posts. She saw it as more of a Bermuda Triangle cataclysm kinda thing.

I'd always thought of myself as an equal opportunity mocker spreading my sarcasm in an egalitarian way. But maybe I'm an opportunist mocker who takes advantage of poor, defenseless, absurd situations. Wait. Aren't they the same thing? Maybe I'm bi-opportunal. I'd need to fast to find the true answer that lies in my soul. So I guess I'll never know. She was entitled to her opinion and I to mine.

~

Three months later, I sat at a cafe with some water and an exceptionally small shared raspberry tart across the table from my accuser. She remained a reader of my blog for quite some time. Until I referred to the new Egyptian regime as Islamist. Which offended her even though that was how the mainstream media referred to it. Whatever. Before all that, she e-mailed me a few times and wanted to meet in person to tell me something important. She was in town for just one day; could we get together?

I was completely intrigued. Meeting someone I didn't know who thought I'd insulted her religion at a cafe shrouded in mystery? Yes, please! Although I was pretty sure I'd solved the mystery before I even got there. I collected my thoughts, did some research and considered my moral obligation. I knew what I had to do. I just didn't want to do it. Because it involved talking and confrontation. Specifically, talking and confronting someone who was already a bit familiar with me from my writing and a bit critical of me from my writing. And I didn't know much about her at all.

She was a gorgeous, blue-eyed blonde in her early thirties who'd recently converted to Islam and moved to Morocco a few months shy of a year before. She told a romantic story of having found Islam in L.A. where she'd worked in the TV industry. She'd fallen in love with the purity of the religion. She gave up the fast life partying with celebrities to pursue her quest to be closer to god, which of course involved fasting. She sold most of her belongings and moved from the land of milk and honey to the land of goat milk and even more honey by herself. She taught herself Darija and read the Koran religiously. I was completely captivated by her adventurous story and her passion was contagious. And we haven't even gotten to the passionate part yet.

"What do your parents think about you moving to Morocco?" I asked.

"They're totally supportive. They miss having me in the States. They worry about me. But we Skype a lot." Then she told me, "I was at the Ministry of Foreign Affairs filing paperwork today."

I knew this from an e-mail she'd sent earlier. I'd googled the kind of paperwork you do there.

"I'm going to marry a Moroccan man."

That was exactly what I'd deduced but pretended I hadn't and feigned surprise. "Congratulations! What does everyone back home say?"

I'd heard this story a million times with a million different details but it was still the same story. Girl meets boy, knows him for a month or two, everything is rainbows and butterflies, they wait until they're married to have sex so they rush to get married and start their wonderful blissful problem-free life together. This was the passion part, where urgency and lust ruled the brain.

Thinking with your head can't be rushed. It took time, discipline, and the quelling of throbbing body parts, maybe going solo for a while, if you know what I mean. And, of course, also considering how much lust a foreigner might have for your green card. Not that true love doesn't happen despite a person's Americanism but lots of times, that's exactly what did happen. I'd heard enough tragic Peace Corps volunteer stories to confirm this phenomenon.

The average American marriage had a fifty percent chance of survival. The chance of a transnational marriage surviving was even worse. I looked it up in the name of research for our meeting. The thing about rainbows and butterflies is they're fleeting. Sometimes even a unicorn quotient was involved where everything was a complete mirage from the beginning. It's not that the odds can't be beaten; it's just that the odds are you won't be the one to do it. Even if you manage to stay married, it's undeniably miserable, at least parts of it.

Hopefully, the crap is counterbalanced by peaks of happy-ishness through the years. Married couples who tell you differently are either lying, newlyweds, or using heavy narcotics. Maybe all three. The unromantic reality is that love isn't nearly enough to make a marriage work. That's why there's a legal contract involved. 'Cause it's so much easier to leave riding on a unicorn in search of a pot of gold somewhere else when it turns out reality doesn't compare to the fantasy.

I knew all this because I'd been married almost twenty years. To the perfect man. He's kind, intelligent, humble, giving, industrious, funny, supportive, diligent, steadfast, good-looking, a good provider and a fantastic dad. From the outside, we appear to be the success story of marital bliss. We're not. We've both wanted to bail at some point. Early in our marriage, Craig wanted out. Because I'm not the easiest person to be in a relationship with, let alone a relationship that's supposed to last a lifetime. Because I stonewalled him from my most intimate and emotional thoughts. I'd always been an impenetrable fortress.

Most recently I wanted out. Because we didn't seem to have a connection anymore; we merely lived individual lives under the same roof. Because of all that shit I hadn't done earlier in our marriage to form a truly intimate relationship. That's why I felt an obligation as an old married woman to tell this love-naive stranger the harsh truth. Because I was the cautionary tale. That and because I was one of the few people in country she knew who spoke English.

Right before we met, while we were on the phone trying to pin down which cafe we were meeting at near which McDonalds, the first red flag went up.

"I'm traveling with a man," she said. "So when we meet, act like we're old friends. I'll explain later."

"OK," I said. 'Cause how else do you respond to that?

Her fiancé accompanied her on the long trip from the south of the country up to Rabat, the capital, where they'd filed papers for their impending wedding.

"He doesn't know about my blog," she said. "Or that I work. Or that I'm writing a book. So I told him you were an old friend from the States."

Three more flags. Did she hear herself? She had to know how bad that sounded, right? How couldn't she? I wanted to lay it all out. A nice, perfect sanitized version of everything I was thinking while skipping over the part about my own marriage because she was a volatile acquaintance at best and I hadn't even shared the details of my on-the-rocks marriage with my closest friends.

I didn't though. I didn't do anything. Instead I chose to be Switzerland, at least on the exterior. Inside my head I was shouting, *Caution! Red flags everywhere! Save yourself! Get out now!* Unfortunately, it was completely inaudible to her. I have no idea how because it was extremely loud in my head and the din rumbled and echoed for days afterward.

She was so talkative I couldn't get a word in edgewise, so it was easy to rationalize my inaction. It's not that I expected she'd change her plans based on anything I said anyway. If everyone she knew was happy for her, why would she listen to a total stranger with a bad attitude? What would have been the point? So I could be a douchebag who says I told you so later? That wasn't what I wanted. So I didn't say anything. Instead I wished her well even though my gut, the eternal cynic, said they were doomed.

While I was abominable at speaking my mind in person, writing thoughts down was a different story entirely. That was my optimal medium for communication and contemplation. It helped that writing gave me time to marinate my thoughts and edit them several times over before anyone else saw them. I had begun to reveal myself and in doing so began, much to my surprise, to accept myself. Not for the perfect person I'd always aspired to be but for the flawed, imperfect blunderer I was. The bonus being that in writing, I could insulate my insecurities with a thick layer of humor.

Moroccan culture came with the expectation that women should be conservative and demure. It was true that Morocco was far more liberal than neighboring countries. Still, it was home to brutal and archaic laws. One caused a sixteen-year-old Moroccan girl to commit suicide by ingesting rat poison. To avoid the ruling of a judge who sentenced her twenty-six-year-old rapist the punishment of marrying her. And yes, you read that correctly.

While Morocco had a friendly girl-next-door image, it harbored a dirty little secret: women were still separate and not nearly equal. Especially if they were unfortunate enough to have been born poor. Poverty severely reduced the likelihood that a woman would receive an education. Especially rural women, whose illiteracy rate was a whopping 90 percent. As a foreign-born educated woman with access to the internet and who was irreverent to the unwritten Moroccan code of proper women's conduct, I could write about it all with relative anonymity. Even though I always wrote under my own name, no one knew me. Or so I thought.

My blog had developed its own readership but was still statistically insignificant in the blogosphere. I never made money from it. I didn't have sponsors. And I didn't know who was reading what I wrote. Which was the whole point of a blog—having the courage to put yourself in front of an audience blindfolded, standing naked for the whole world to see. It's very peep show-ish. People caught glimpses and felt they knew me even though they didn't.

I never wrote to please the reader. That was just a happy accident that happened along the journey. My content was determined by whatever I felt like writing whenever the hell I felt like writing it. The only grappling I had with the blog and my conscious was where to draw the line with what was too personal to share publicly, especially where my family was concerned.

~

Belly dance continued to be dreadfully uncomfortable. And by that I mean I had to force myself to go only to stand awkwardly while the other women chitchatted in Darija. While chastising myself for not remembering the steps. My mind abandoned my body when I danced and not in a carefree, lost in the moment, dance with reckless abandon kind of way. My mind ruminated on how painful it was to be exposed and my stiff body recoiled.

I was defective. Many classes I spent all my energy willing myself not to walk out or burst into tears. Because the music, combined with movement stirred them all up for some reason. So, I resorted to old defense mechanisms and pretended no one could see me in the back of the room. But being tall by Moroccan standards, extremely thin, glowingly pale, and singled out by instructor Zeinab, who referred to me as Nicole Kidman, made invisibility impossible. I had to make peace with consuming space, being seen, and feeling entitled to do so. While dance looked fun for everyone else, it was laborious and painful for me. I forced myself to go twice a week anyway. The goal being that one day I would have the courage to do it on stage in front of people no matter how imperfect I was.

I didn't have that opportunity in Morocco. There was no recital at the end of the year. Belly dance there wasn't for public consumption, except for tourists. Women danced for each other in private, women danced for their husbands in private, but women didn't dance in front of other women's husbands or in public. Doing so came with the stigma of being a slut or a prostitute. Zeinab told me that in the rusty English of her youth. She'd been forced to change languages many times as Egypt itself had changed. Somewhere along the line, I'd forgotten she was a foreign woman there often bewildered by the local culture too.

Since I didn't have a forum for dancing, I began videotaping myself dancing alone in my own home on the days our man-maid Mohammed didn't work. Not because I thought I was a good dancer, but because I thought I was an atrocious one. I'd always felt like a quiet disaster on the inside. And I wanted out of my own insecurities and perfectionism. I wanted to see me the way the rest of the world saw me, from the outside. To reveal myself for what I truly was—desperately uncoordinated and completely imperfect.

I judged myself so hard, just hitting the button on the video camera alone sent me into heart palpitations. Even though I was alone and could just delete it; no one would be the wiser. Then I took it a step further. And posted the footage on youtube to import into my blog. That's where I got supportive comments from armchair belly dance connoisseurs. "You must give a great blow job, cause your dancing really sucks!"

Being bad mouthed by an anonymous jerk off seeking to twerk off wasn't the reason I started taking another dance class. I did that because Sara was teaching it. Hiding in the back wasn't an option here. It was a very small group and it was at my house by a professional dancer and certified dance therapist. The latter came as a shock to me. Dance therapy? What could be more ridiculously stupid?

Then it hit me. All the writing, working out and dancing? I'd been self-medicating and hadn't realized it. Maybe dance wasn't frivolous at all and all those activities meant more to me than I'd thought. They made me stronger, braver, and ultimately more accepting of myself.

As much as it pains me to say it, my therapists were right. I lacked self-esteem. And because I had none, I racked up a long history of prioritizing everyone else's needs above mine. My specialty had been catering to the toxic people who'd come and gone over the years. At certain points, I neglected the healthy people in my life like Craig, the elements and my close friends to rescue them. I was their self-deprecating sidekick, funder, confidant, enabler, faithful servant and most of all, their tool.

They'd earned all that through buttloads of guilt and manipulation. Those had always been the keys to my heart; they'd always worked their magic on me. Red flags had been there all along, I just hadn't seen them until now. After countless hours of therapy and even more internet research about emotional vampires, suddenly I saw them for the destructive distractions they truly were.

I was determined to terminate them from my life. To refocus on the true priorities, my family and the good friends who'd always supported me. And, of course, me and my needs. I needed to stop being a third person in my own life.

As I was trying to fix my own craziness and ward off sociopaths, I realized I was doing it in a world chock full of sociopaths.

## THE SOCIOPATH NEXT DOOR

My next door neighbor was a sociopath. Not only was he an evil dictator who committed numerous crimes against humanity, he also committed numerous crimes of fashion by emulating Michael Jackson. And he didn't pull it off well, by the way.

Yeah, Muammar Gaddafi lived east of my house, a straight shot down the road just past the goat farm on the left. And now he's dead. One less sociopath in the world. But do you know how many sociopaths there are in the world? Do you?

First, I must confess that my order from Amazon.com finally arrived. So I've been a reading fiend of late. One of my latest reads? You guessed it. It's titled *The Sociopath Next Door.* And how fitting is that when I actually did live next to a sociopath? I am veritable neighbors to a few: Gaddafi, Mubarak and Bin Laden. How does this affect you, you ask? Because you live near a sociopath too. I guarantee it.

How do I know this? Because 1 in 25 people are sociopaths. I'm not a math whiz or anything but that's like 4% of the population, right? Now I know you're thinkin' whhhhhhaaaaaaaatttt? This can't be true. The thing is not all sociopaths are terrorists, dictators or murders. They're everyday people who don't have a conscience. None. So they can do anything they want without guilt or remorse.

What does your run of the mill sociopath do? They thrive on power, wealth and conquest. In your neighborhood, that could mean they're the president of your HOA, your therapist, your minister, the cop, or the room mom for your kid's third-grade class who always gives you that creepy vibe. They drain bank accounts, your accomplishments, self-esteem, and peace on earth. (That is a semi-plagiaristic, semi-altered quote from the book. And I don't even care. OK, I totally care. That's why I confessed. See, I can't find the page number that I got it from to go back and quote it properly and I'm totally riddled with guilt. I'm obviously not a sociopath.)

Now, I know exactly what you're doing right now. 'Cause I did the same thing. You're going down the list of people you know. And you're putting them into categories: definitely not a sociopath, definitely a sociopath, and oh-my-god-that-explains-so-much-o-path! Because there are people on the escarpments of our everyday lives who want in so they can exert power and control. Oh, they will pretend that they care about you but they have no capacity for love or attachment.

OK, so this is that weird segue in the post where I reveal exactly how nerdy I am. (As if you don't know by now.) So I was watching this *20/20* episode on YouTube that was based on the book *The Gift of Fear* by Gavin de Becker. Remember that creepy vibe I mentioned earlier about the third-grade room mom? We all have that instinctual creepy vibe that informs us we're in danger. Even if we can't clearly see what the threat is, we feel that something's not right. Our respect for authority figures, our ability to overthink situations, wait for evidence and just plain being polite allows us to negate the threat. Thus we become susceptible to friendly neighborhood sociopaths who are natural-born charmers even if they're not natural-born killers. Isn't that fascinating?

So maybe you don't live next to Jeffrey Dahmer and chances are that's because he's dead. But you do have a sociopath in your life. We all do. What can you do to protect yourself? First, I would recommend not moving to Iran or North Korea. Get in touch with your creepy vibe. Don't feel guilty for being suspicious about your new neighbor Fred Bundy who has a penchant for having beautiful women over to his house late at night who strangely never appear to leave. And for god's sake, the next time Suzie's mom, the creepy room mom, brings those beautiful special family recipe chocolate cupcakes to the Halloween party, make sure your kid doesn't eat one!

*Addendum: After its original debut on my blog, I received the most powerful private message from a reader. In reading my post, she came to the heartbreaking realization that her grown son was indeed a sociopath.*

# *Chapter 14*

# Go Ahead, Deport Me

The elements' morale was waning. They didn't like their school and they didn't like being forced to entertain themselves because there was nothing to do. They abhorred the smells in the medina. Marjane didn't sell the latest or greatest anything. The only things to like were the beach and travel. Specifically, travel outside Morocco. So that technically didn't qualify as something the elements liked about Morocco. Unless you said they liked getting out of it.

Despite their bad-mouthing, they possessed a contentment they'd never achieved in the States. They didn't spend their days wanting; they spent them imagining and making up their own games. Because they had to. When we discovered there was a reality TV show set in Morocco, I grabbed the chance to rub in how fortunate we were.

"See how cool it is?" I crowed. "Aren't we lucky to live here?"

They didn't know that virtually everything has its own reality TV show in the States so seeing one about Morocco didn't make it special. There were shows about catfish, for god's sake. The good thing about not having TV was being spared hours of wasting my life watching someone else live theirs. Especially if there was a six-year-old girl competing in beauty pageants or anyone fishing, ever.

Once in a while, we found something worth watching. But downloading it from the internet required hours of preplanning, sometimes a whole day. The only thing we could get on demand in Morocco was frustration. Unless we counted irritation, disappointment, annoyance, dissatisfaction and chagrin separately. Because inevitably when we'd found something worthy of watching, the stream to users outside the U.S. was blocked. Then my friend Linda told me about *Expedition Impossible*, a show where teams raced through Morocco. Somehow we beat the odds and got to see it illegally through other channels.

I'd always felt kinda like an outcast in America. I didn't watch sports, I had no desire to go to Vegas, I'd never bought a lottery ticket, I wasn't a natural-born hugger, I hate wearing shorts and I didn't follow which celebrity was in rehab on any given week because I couldn't have cared less. So I loved living where no one talked about the previous night's episode of *The Bachelor.* Even though it was blasted across Facebook the next morning.

Expats for the most part tended to be foreigners to American popular culture. Not that we didn't have our individual ties to American things. Sara got up in the middle of the night to watch the Super Bowl with her husband. Christopher reciprocated by getting up way too early (or late, depending on how you look at it) to watch the Royal Wedding. Kim and her husband Bob got out of bed to listen to baseball on the radio. Yes, listen, on the radio, without any boring baseball visuals even, which was surely a better sleep aid than Ambien could ever be.

Expats might mention that kind of stuff in passing but there was no water cooler play by play. No cashier would make idle chitchat with the ever-popular, "Some game last night, huh?" I still don't know who won the Super Bowl, who played, or even more important by American standards, who performed the halftime show. And if someone's boob popped out during it or not. No one dwelled on that kind of stuff overseas.

The only truly dwell-able topics were politics, food, and travels that brought those things together in what was the perfect marriage. Like the time I was raped by the Euro in London while eating a pot-pie I'd assumed was chicken but instead had been packed with organ meats. England had never been on the list of places I wanted to go, and I'd written off eating liver after years of being forced to choke it down piled high with onions as a kid. 'Cause both of my parents were terminally shy liver-loving freaks. So what could make me suddenly change my mind? Two magic words. CHEAP TICKETS. By cheap, I mean bargain-basement cheap. From Morocco to London, for six people, all for the low, low price of $600! It's true.

Craig was in Tanzania when I found the tickets and had the England epiphany. When I called to tell him, he was all like, "You don't want to go to England, remember?" And I was all like, "It's $600, remember?" Fighting me on this was fruitless because in addition to being terminally shy myself, I was also terminally stubborn. Did I mention he's the most patient man ever? He has to be. He's married to me.

I took his silence as an indication that he was totally on board with London. So I got off the phone and bought the tickets. I would have been a fool not to. When Craig returned from his work trip and checked his inbox, the flight itinerary was waiting. Being the thorough proofreader he was, he noticed the problem immediately. It was missing something.

The return trip.

Thus explaining why I'd gotten such a great deal. Because being the skim through the details moron that I was, I'd bought six nonrefundable one-way tickets to a place I didn't even want to go.

We arrived at the Stansted airport way out in the middle of a cow field nowhere near London at midnight. We waited before we paced around a bit then called Tammy's number. Craig had found Tammy on the internet. She'd rented us an apartment and arranged for a driver to meet us. Or she was supposed to. Now that we were there, he couldn't get through on her number. Right about then we started to get suspicious that the really cheap accommodations Craig had made on the internet in zone 1 that had seemed too good to be true really were. Welcome to international travel Loerzel style where nothing goes as planned and every trip is a complete and total flippin' trip.

Desperate for sleep, we scrambled and found a much too expensive place close to the airport. The next two days were spent trying to find cheaper accommodations for the rest of the week and trying to get ahold of Scammy Tammy. That's when I did something I normally don't do on vacation. I checked my e-mail. In addition to several annoying notifications from the kids' school that their lunch accounts were low and I should add more dirhams immediately, my big brother Jim had sent me a message. He was going to be in London the following day for just one night. When we'd lived in Germany, I used to see him every other month whenever he copiloted the Frankfurt flight. Since we'd moved Stateside, then to Africa, I hadn't seen him in a few years. He said he would call Craig's cell when he got to the hotel.

The next day, we visited the Natural History Museum. No call. On to the outdoor ice skating rink. Nothing. We finally decided to head back to the apartment to check our e-mail. The flight had been delayed, he'd slept for a couple of hours after he'd arrived and tried to call us but hadn't been able to get through. We left a message at his hotel but he was out and about exploring the city somewhere completely unreachable because his cell phone didn't accept international calls. We're both minimalistic technotards that way only I don't fly a plane, thank god. But it was already late. We were finally in the same city at the same time and we'd missed each other!

The trip all went so fast the way it does when you're traveling somewhere that boasts an abundance of public trashcans and people who use them. We'd only seen our friends Claire and Keith, who were coincidentally on the same flight to London, for a brief lunch. When their son got sick, that foiled the plans we'd made to get together again. There was still so much to see and do. We faced the pressure of the last day of vacation by brutally editing what we wanted to see compared to what was achievable by mere mortals with four kids in tow. Should we go to a museum? Go shopping? See the Tower of London? Go out for fish and chips? Yeah, all of that.

On the way to the Victoria and Albert Museum, we detoured at King's Cross station. It was home to platform 9 3/4 from Harry Potter fame. Well, it used to be, anyway. We searched the entire station and couldn't find it. Then we asked. They'd moved it outside where it had become merely a niche next to the road where it wouldn't impede the bustling London tube traffic. A huge disappointment, especially considering this tube stop was nowhere near our apartment or where we were going that day.

As we make our way to the Victoria and Albert Museum, we walked through the shopping district. Our pace slowed to a saunter. It was November and the store windows were decorated for Christmas complete with falling snowflakes. It was so familiar and nostalgic, it felt like home. When we finally made it to the museum, I was immediately captivated by a handblown glass chandelier above the reception desk.

"I bet you anything that's a Chihuly," I told Craig, who knew better than to bet me on anything like that. I don't bet often, but when I do, your best bet is that I'm right.

We chatted with the docent about the piece and she confirmed it was a Chihuly and I felt all self-righteous and art snobbish.

"Maa-rie!" a familiar voice called from directly behind me.

Brother Jim! His flight back to the States left later than he'd thought, so he'd come to the museum to kill some time thinking maybe he'd bump into us. In a city of more than 7 million people, what were the chances of being in the same place at the same time? When Jim relayed the details of the previous day, we discovered we'd gone to the same exact places but had missed each other by about half an hour.

We had about an hour and a half before he needed to leave for the airport. We walked through the museum while catching up. The elements fought for Uncle Jim's attention and barraged him with questions. I'd gotten so distracted by our travels I hadn't realized how much I missed friends and family back home and how I'd unintentionally neglected them. Time flew and before we knew it, it was time for Jim to take off again.

~

When we returned home, I realized we only had seven short months left in Morocco. They would go by quickly. Soon I would trade neglect of my American friends for neglect of my Moroccan ones.

It was hard to believe our tour of duty was almost up. The first year had crawled by so slowly while we'd adjusted to Moroccan life, made friends, developed routines and learned how to get things done in Africa. Until we cultivated a true understanding of Moroccan life and accepted that many things just don't get done at all. We were over the hump and there was no slowing this donkey cart down. We'd be saying goodbyes again way to soon. To our friends, the chaos and the smell of burning goat heads.

Soon we'd be bored in boring Colorado. Craig would return to his same practice where he was a partner and we'd kick out our renters and live in the same house. Though hopefully we wouldn't resort to living the same way. Hopefully, Craig would work fewer hours and be home to help more. Hopefully, I'd be more appreciative and communicative when he did.

I was devoted to returning with a new focus. To be completely selfish by putting myself first, a commitment to put my family second. And good friends third. That bumped them up the list after I eliminated extraneous distractions like dumping time into needy acquaintances who didn't really like me anyway. I no longer needed their superficial approval. I was rededicating myself to being the best friend I could to the people who really had been my best friends all along.

Maybe I'd arrive home to those reprioritized friends earlier than expected. If I got us deported. About ten days before we left for London, I'd written a blog post about the King of Morocco.

"I got called into Peggy's office today," Craig told me after we'd safely tucked the elements into bed. Peggy was the country director of the Peace Corps in Morocco and Craig's boss.

"For what?" I asked.

"About your post 'The King and I,'" he said.

"What? Why? Wait. She knows I have a blog?"

No one at the Peace Corps knew about my blog.

"Well, she does now. Someone at the U.S. Embassy called her about it."

"Well, it was pretty funny. Is she friends with someone from the embassy who told her about it?"

Considering we live in the bubble, that was a stupid question.

"The Embassy called Peggy to have her talk to me so I could ask you to take the post down."

This was turning into a middle-school version of the telephone game. Which led me to believe that the original message might have been *I love that clown* instead of *take it down*. Next we'd be necking in a closet playing spin the bottle.

"So why did they ask you and not me?" I asked.

"Because you don't work for the government. So they don't have a say in what you do."

"Exactly! Thank god for that! I'm not taking it down, especially now. I don't care that it's illegal to make fun of the King. That shit was funny. And true. And that whole notion that he can't be criticized, it's wrong and really stupid just like the King." I thought for a second. "Wait a minute. Do you want me to take it down?"

"No! It's hilarious!"

"What if this affects your job? What if you get fired? What if... they deport us?"

"I don't care about losing my job or leaving Morocco. What matters is us. Plus, I make more money in the States, remember? Don't take it down!"

"Oh my god, wouldn't being deported be the perfect ending of Rock The Kasbah ever? The attention could help jumpstart my writing career! Go ahead, deport me!"

We didn't know what would happen next and we didn't ask. Nor did I send Craig with a note for Peggy to take to the Embassy to ask who the hell had asked me to take it down in the first place. I figured I was better off not knowing. So, I just spread suspicion onto people I didn't like anyway rather than discover it had been someone I liked who turned out to be an Embassy automaton.

I'd already met too many people there I thought were friends before they slowly revealed themselves to be foes. When you live in a bubble and you're a compulsive liar, eventually you get caught. I didn't want to take the risk of investing any more time, energy and trust into anyone new. Or any old acquaintances, only to be brutishly disappointed.

Because of the post, Craig thought we might have some trouble getting back into Morocco on our way home from London. We didn't. In fact, nothing happened. Nothing at all. And that totally pissed me off! I was angsty and frustrated and I desperately wanted to take it out on someone. I was ready to rumble and take them down. All of them. Well, except that body builder guy at the embassy I was sure was taking steroids. All I needed was a ring. And fuck it all, I wouldn't get that.

## THE KING AND I

**Every business in Morocco has one. And no, it's not a business license. Most homes have one too. And no, it's not a bathroom.**

'Cause plenty of houses still don't have bathrooms here. What do they have instead? A picture of King Mohammed VI.

I know what you're thinking. *With all the revolutions in North Africa, Morocco is still ruled by a King?* Yes, it is. Oh, there was an election in July of this year to curb some of his powers. But, the elections were controversial and even though his power is reduced, he still controls the armed forces, the judiciary and foreign policy. He's also kept the role of religious leader too. But, that's not what this post is about.

It's about those pictures of him. The thing is, there isn't just one official picture of the King in circulation. There are different versions in a wide variety of poses, angles, formal and unconvincingly informal shots. So no matter what your business, you can have a picture of the King that somehow endorses your business or reflects your outlook on life. Here are just some of your choices:

LEGAL DISCLAIMER: MY LAWYER SAYS I CAN'T INCLUDE COPIES OF THE PHOTOS HERE. SO YOU'LL JUST HAVE TO USE YOUR IMAGINATION OR GOOGLE MY DESCRIPTIONS TO SEE FOR YOURSELF.

Here's the King drinking a super sugary glass of traditional Moroccan tea in a suit and tie.
How Western of him.

I saw this particular photo in a restaurant. I personally think it would be great to hang in a dentist's office with all that sugar. Not that most Moroccans go to the dentist. That being the point.

This one is the King standing in front of his throne looking very official but with a contorted face like he's on the verge of puking up his lunch.

Personally, I think this really humanizes the King. This would be a great choice for doctor's offices and the meat kebab guy. Really anyplace where unrefrigerated food is sold and exposed to stray cats. So really, everywhere. I figure this one is probably a top seller for just that reason.

He's in some religious garb here with a big white padded bonnet on.

He looks like a Q-tip. The perfect choice for baby supply stores, cosmetics counters and costume shops. Not that there are costume shops here.

The King kneeling beside a deer wearing a Moroccan looking poncho and cowboy hat while the dead deer bleeds from its mouth.

This is my personal favorite...deer huntin' King. As if he took down that buck! Come on, he had one his emissaries do the dirty work for him. Maybe he could take down a doe, I mean a buck, on the Wii version, which is why I think this should be on the wall of an electronics store. Although I found this picture on the wall of a film store obviously advertising for Photoshop.

Oh, there are so many other ridiculous official photos of the King. They all fascinate and amuse me. I'd never really thought about where people got these pictures before. That was until I saw a stack of them at Aswak Assalam, a local grocery store. And I was so freakin' excited. Like way too freakin' excited because I'd never seen them for sale anywhere before. And I knew I had to have one of my very own!

So I perused the selection and there was one, just one, of my first choice left. Yessss! I put it in my crappy cart with the bad wheel, finished shopping and headed to the cashier. The young woman rang up my purchases but the picture didn't have a price tag. She called for assistance. *Price check, aisle 6!*

Three phone calls and ten minutes later, someone finally came. They look at the picture then go to the stack. None of them are priced. That guy calls another guy. They deliberate and inform the cashier they can't sell it because they don't know the price. Whh-hhaaaaaaatttttt? I thought this was a store and the goal is to sell stuff. Right? The fact that they would just choose not to sell it is so freakin' stupid that now I'm freakin' pissed.

So I go back into the aisles to get the attention of the pricing guys or a manager, which doesn't work. They ignore me. I head back to the cashier, the only person who's attention I can get and ask her to get someone. I tell her it's ridiculous that no one will help me. Don't they want to sell the picture? Why can't you just make up a price? Someone will sell me one off their own wall at the medina!

But I'm gabbering on in English so she has no idea what I'm saying. And as my friend Sara says, it's not what you say, it's the tone you say it in. And mine isn't friendly. All she knows is I'm a crazy foreign lady who won't leave her line. I know I'm intimidating her. Yesssssssss! I feel guilty using her as my pawn. I wouldn't do things this way in the States but then again I wouldn't have to do this in the States.

Finally, after half an hour standoff in the checkout line and another two price guy later...

I won! I won! I won!

I now have my very own picture of the King hanging in the entryway. He's wearing red fake Ray Bans with an off-white djellaba and a fez cap and he's waving. I think this picture totally says cool casual King. Or, you could say, the future's so bright I gotta wear shades King. But I think that would be completely inaccurate. And I'm especially glad I got the last one before he's gone. I mean, it's gone. Of course.

# Chapter 15

## Stunt Girl in a Burka

I am the youngest of six kids, born a blond and a stunt girl. Oddly, I was a desperately quiet, timid kid who loved to entertain people. Usually this was done by somersaulting through the middle of the living room for our guests. In our big Catholic family we all looked like miniature versions of my dad, so I longed to stand out. I took any attention that came my way because, with seven other people in the house, it didn't come my way very often.

As a textbook youngest child, I usually got it by being the clown. Since I was also intuitive, I knew exactly when to disappear because dad was in a mood or mom was doling out chores. I still have impeccable timing for avoidance. My three big brothers also taught me that size doesn't matter; kicking a boy in the balls won every fight every time. That's how I also knew I have impeccable aim. The blond was nature, the brawn was nurture. I grew into the brunette, right-brained, introverted dreamer who'll make you laugh at her own expense or take you down with a good ninja kick. If you're really unlucky, both.

My stunt career began around the age of six. We were heading home in my family's station wagon after my brothers' baseball game.

Since baseball was the most boring sport in the world, I'd brought my funkadelic plastic paisley '70's purse packed with my pet rock. After the game, my brothers stayed behind for the after party where they would compare grass stains or hold spitting contests or whatever big brothers did.

My sister Kathy and I climbed onto the back bench seat of our puke brown Chevrolet. Mom was speeding down Niagara Falls Boulevard when I leaned against the door. The one I hadn't shut properly. The door opened and dumped me out effortlessly. I landed on the unyielding asphalt in the middle of a busy thoroughfare. This was before seatbelt laws when lap belts were just a weapon to smack your brother with.

There I was in the fast lane with my springy blond pigtails, bearing a striking resemblance to Drew Barrymore in ET, dodging Saturday afternoon traffic and sprinting after my mom's car. She didn't show any signs of stopping. My Jackie Chan action sequence seemed to have been choreographed on mute. Maybe that's why my mom hadn't noticed. Or maybe she didn't care. She did have five other kids. I was replaceable. Popping out another one was just another Tuesday at the hospital eating her beloved liver and onions with a side of lime Jell-O.

My sister Kathy shouted, "Stop! Marie fell out of the car!"

But since she was the loudmouth who never stopped talking, my mom just ignored her. Everyone did. When Mom finally checked the rearview mirror, probably just to give Kathy the look, she saw me racing down the four-lane road clutching my purse like a football.

She pulled into a mall parking lot. I climbed right back in like nothing had happened. Except for my bloody knees, I was relatively unscathed. The purse my grandma had given me had a huge brush burn on one side. I'd never seen my mom cry before so I didn't know what to make of it. After all, I was totally fine. It was my Bionic Woman moment. I'd spent hours in the yard pretending to be her prepping for an opportunity to magically become her making bionic sounds and totally committing to character. Some athleticism and malleable bones that should have broken many times over, like when I'd fallen twenty feet from a tree house that collapsed on top of me, didn't hurt either.

As a tomboy, I loved being outside riding my bike, skating, making worm farms, playing catch with my brothers, and adventuring way past the perimeters of wherever I was supposed to be often with kids I was forbidden to play with. My knees and elbows were constantly bruised and scrapped. I even stepped on an upturned rusty nail that went clear through my sneaker and into my foot during a game of hide and seek. I didn't utter a sound or go crying to my mommy. No way would I give away my hiding spot! I wanted to win!

Even though I was an easygoing kid, I was also extremely sensitive and self-conscious. A total people pleaser, which was at odds with my need to explore, which always got me in trouble. Especially the lying to cover my tracks. I was consumed with what everyone thought of me and desperately wanted to fit in. Except I couldn't follow the rules. Mishaps and mistakes seemed to follow me. I never seemed to fit in and I felt defective. And I knew that if people knew the real me, they wouldn't like me.

I wanted to be perfect. That way I wouldn't get into trouble anymore and everyone around me would live in peace and harmony. That would also ensure I wouldn't get spanked again. And I don't mean the modern Urban Dictionary definition of spanked where you're about to make a post on an internet forum and someone beats you to the punch kind of spanked. That's when an idealist-perfectionist was born.

My twenties were spent in college, volunteering, working part-time jobs and full-time jobs, and eventually becoming a professional in the social work field. Where I could do my do-gooding and make everyone happy like a Coke commercial where everyone knows the same song, a flash mob starts and they form a perfect circle while singing in perfect harmony. Craig and I were newly married. He was in medical school and I was in grad school and working full-time and part-time jobs to make ends meet. We were both so busy we rarely saw each other. If we did, we were wearing the classic 90's college uniform of Umbro soccer shorts and big baggy t-shirts with our faces stuffed in textbooks. The '90's weren't a sexy decade.

In my thirties, I became a mother when we adopted the elements. We'd tried for so long to have kids and I wanted to be a mom more than anything. I gladly gave up my career. Days were spent changing blown-out poopy diapers, picking up Play-Doh crumbs from all corners of the house, and enforcing and reinforcing that playing dog with the jumprope tied around your sisters' neck is unsafe. That was a particularly frequent issue until I finally threw out the damn jumpropes and any extra shoelaces.

. When I wasn't exhausted and feeling like the world's crappiest mom, because that's just what us mom's do, every once in a while I felt like I was missing something. I always felt that way, like there was a hole that nothing and nobody could fill.

Except me.

~

I'd been writing the blog for over a year. I started too many sentences And, Or, and Except. I posted videos of me belly dancing craptastically for the whole world to see. I got hate mail and didn't hate it. I was displaying the real me for the first time in my life. For years I'd felt like I was chasing my mom's car down the middle of the boulevard. I'd finally figured out how to fill the hole. And it had been so stinkin' simple all along. All I needed to do was be me and do what I really wanted to do. Which was everything.

Mostly I wanted to connect with other people, especially women. Having always been a tomboy, I'd never spent much time thinking about what it meant to be a woman. Until I travelled and saw how fortunate I was to be an American and a female. To be educated, have equal rights, and not be forced to marry my rapist. I wanted a global view of what it meant to be a woman, to see how life would be if I'd been born into a completely different culture. I was on a mission and I didn't care how stupid it seemed. Bionic sound effects might come in handy.

~

My friend and I went to the medina on a quest. We inquired at shops that sold *djellabas*. We stopped at scarf stores. Everywhere the answer was the same: If you want a burka in Morocco, you must make your own.

This was the first indication that I wasn't going to get that embroidered burka hand-stitched by a women's co-op up in the mountains. Dammit. It seemed really wrong to pay a tailor, many of whom were men, to sew a burka for me. I won't be put in a burka at a man's hand, only my own. I didn't care if that was sexist, reverse sexist or whatever. I am woman, hear me roar. So I took to the internet.

And that's how I discovered there are some really expensive blinged-out burkas. Which seemed to defeat the purpose of modesty with a burka in the first place. But I'm on a burka budget. After hours of surfing several different sites, I ordered from eBay. It seemed safer than ordering a burka online from Iran. Then I realized I have no idea what size burka I wear. The one I chose didn't come in small, medium and large. It came in sizes like 54, 56, 58 and 60. Inches? Head to ankle? Shoulder to foot? I have no idea. Pick a number. Any number. Click. Done.

It took over a month to arrive. All 100% polyester of it, factory made in India, of all places. Probably by a relative of the guy I called about the Scammy Tammy credit card fraud. The head covering doesn't look anything like the picture that made it appear to be one piece that simply plopped on top of the head like a Kentucky Derby hat. It looked kind of like a KKK hood. But no, it was one big square of fabric with a separate veil for the face and it didn't come with instructions. This would require research, which I liked. And skill, which I seriously lacked.

Back to the internet. I searched for burka images. The first picture that popped up? Yup, a naked woman. Well, not totally naked. She's wearing an exquisite *hijab*. I wondered how she tied it. That answered the lifelong question: Does burka porn exist? It does.

The first thing I learned about *hijabs*, the headscarves, was that I'm supposed to wear an under cap over my hair under the scarf. I didn't have one. Second, there were tons of different ways to tie a *hijab*. I needed to investigate, practice, then choose. First was the ever popular turkey gobbler, which was tight around the head with the neck kind of drapey. Two problems arose. Without an under cap, a gap showed my hair. And the black scarf was too large to pull this one off without drowning in a sea of fabric.

Soon I became totally obsessed. I ogled women's headscarves on the street trying to figure out how they folded their *hijabs*. Then I'd go home and try to recreate them. I spotted one I called the ninja *hijab*. It was tight all around the head then wrapped around the neck before being tied off at the back of the neck like a noose. It looked super chic and hip-ninja but it felt claustrophobic.

So I tried the Gap wrap. The scarf was loosely slung over the head, looped under the chin and casually tossed over the shoulder. I think if The Gap started selling *hijabs*, it would be this model, simple and casual in t-shirt fabric for comfort. They'd call it *favorite hijab*. Unfortunately, it left a big chunk of my hair exposed. Damn you, gap!

None would work without a skullcap. And I had no freakin' clue where to get one. Then it popped into my head—a headscarf shop was near my house. So I hopped in the car and headed to the mall, sure they would have exactly what I needed. Except the store was no longer there. It had become a men's store, Steve and Barry's or something. How symbolic was that?

Finally I created one with my own unconventional method, which involved several safety pins, which made me feel a little '80's punkish attitude. My *hijab* was a catastrophe. Craig didn't care. He thought it was kinda sexy. I thought that was kinda sexist.

## DAY IN A BURKA

I've always wondered what it would be like to experience the world from inside a burka. So, when we found out we were moving to Morocco, I wanted to do two things—belly dance and wear a burka. I checked the belly dancing box early. Now we're in our last six months and I still hadn't worn a burka. Until now. I grew more anxious as the day drew near. By coincidence, the day I wore the burka was my forty-second birthday.

Let me first add a disclaimer. Burkas, full-on burkas that conceal the face, aren't common here in Morocco. *Hijabs* (head scarves) and *djellabas* (long flowy robes with a hood...think Obi-Wan Kenobi in Star Wars) are. But even those aren't standard. There is no real standard because Moroccan women have lots of choices and wear every combination of *djellaba* and *hijab*. *Djellaba* and no *hijab*, *hijab* with Western clothes. Many women just wear Western clothes without covering their hair at all. In fact, I saw a lot more burkas in London than I've ever seen in Morocco. But, since I'm probably never going to live in Saudi Arabia and be forced to wear a burka, I'm doing it here and now.

It's a little too late to fuss over the details like my *abaya* (the dress-like component) is a little too small. And even though I've practiced several *hijab* wrapping methods, I can't seem to get it right. Or that my *niqab* (the veil that covers my face) looks imprisoned by my *hijab* because of poor execution. This is the best I can do with my informal YouTube self-tutorial on burka wearing with the pieces I have. I didn't get the burka I'd dreamed of, but it will have to do.

My friend picks me up. I'm all decked out in black except for the pop of color in my shoes, those orange ballet flats I've been dying to wear. I knew just the right occasion would present itself for their debut. Then I accessorized with that green purse I love that just sits in my closet. Since I can't display my personality through clothes or hair, it's all in the accessories and black eyeliner.

My friend took a picture of me before we left. I always have the most awkward smile in photos but I figured it didn't matter if I smiled or not since my face was covered. So I decided to forego the smile altogether. When my friend insisted I smile for the second photo, I did. They say you smile with your eyes but the pictures look exactly the same.

We head out to the mall. We're both nervous and our hearts raced. I know you're wondering if she's in a burka too. She's not. For our covert mission, it's easier to be the one covered. When we arrive in the parking lot, we look at each other, confirm that we're ready, and take deep breaths.

Immediately she notices that my entire body language is different. "It's demure," she says. Even though I'm not consciously doing anything different, I can feel it. I'm amazed she can see the change through what amounts to a Hefty garbage bag. I'm a variant of myself already, so quickly.

It was a long slow walk through the mall and down the escalator. Both of us averted our eyes from other mall goers, uncertain how we'd be received. When we reached our destination, we found a table at the sushi restaurant. What could be more awkward than eating with a veil over your mouth? Eating sushi with chopsticks with a veil over your mouth.

At this point my lack of *hijab* wrapping experience is evident. The *hijab* has become blousy and severely impaires my peripheral vision. I can't see anything going on around me but my friend can. She confirms no one notices me. They notice her but I'm a ghost. As if she's sitting alone. Except for the watchful eye of one older woman who lingers and leers at me. Does she know I'm an impostor? The waiter comes to take our order. Well, my friend's order. He doesn't acknowledge me. She orders for both of us. I'm conspicuously invisible.

The server brings our salads and waters. I make a rookie mistake. I forget to lift my *niqab* to get my bottle to my mouth. If I lift the *niqab* and tilt my head back to drink, I fear I'd dismantle my *hijab*. I'm thirsty but decide it's safer not to drink. Instead, I'll focus on eating.

By this point, my friend and I are both getting a bit bolder. I was starving and she was determined to capture this on film. So she discretely taped me eating with chopsticks on our undercover Anderson Cooper cam. I ended up with far more salad on my lap than in my mouth. But I'm invisible so no one notices. The sushi was much easier to manage but with every bite, the entire *hijab* moved and required readjusting. About halfway through the sushi, the choreographed eating and readjusting routine became too tedious. So, I stopped eating altogether.

This was when I realized that something was different between my friend and I. Even though our conversation was light, the air was heavy and somehow somber. The veil recycled all my hot breath back to me. It was probably just our nerves, I reasoned.

We finished and walked to the ice skating rink. It was my birthday, after all. The rink was closed. Damn it. The mall also has a bowling alley. By this point, I'm not looking to see who's looking as we walk to the bowling alley. It doesn't matter anymore because I can't see any of it. My friend, however, is disturbed that in public, I all but cease to exist. I used to live my life trying to be invisible because it was more comfortable that way. I really had changed because there was nothing comfortable about this. This made me more determined than ever to live my life visible to everyone I valued.

Bowling will help us relax and lighten the mood. I trade my flats for bright, shiny bowling shoes and a hot pink ball. The conversation turns from all things burka related to deeper life stuff. Even though everything was fine, something wasn't right.

My too-small *abaya* inhibited my stride. I took smaller strides to accommodate the burka. I didn't want to trip or rip it but it was inhibiting my mad bowling skills. Which I actually don't have. To really bowl, I had to lift it. After several frames, I worked out a system of striding, lifting my burka then releasing the ball. This added a whole new level of coordination to bowling. I'm not a particularly coordinated person to begin with. Nor am I a good bowler. Which, of course, completely explains why I lost.

I lost something else too.

The next day, I realized what I'd lost in the burka. It wasn't that it made doing things more difficult, which it did. Rather, it took the most important thing away from me—my expressions. As a person who isn't particularly good at talking, who has a dry sarcastic wit, my face conveys far more than my words ever could. I contort it to show my cynicism, bite my lip when I feel unsure, squint my eyes to show empathy. And no, I'm not related to Renee Zellweger. As far as I know, anyway.

Our words can lie but our faces and body language don't. So the whole time my friend and I were talking, each of us was only getting half the conversation. That changed the way we interacted. The whole experience was so much more profound than I can put into words. But if you see me in person and ask me about it, you'll see the whole story in my face.

On the way home, I was itching to get out of the burka. We didn't even make it home before I stripped it off while my friend was driving. I didn't think anyone was more relieved than me until I took off the last layer. Looking at my friend, it was clear that she was even more relieved. It was one of the most intimate moments of my life. With a huge smile to welcome me back, she said, "There's my friend."

And just like that, I ceased to be invisible anymore.

# Chapter 16

## Man vs. Wild

It was hard to catch the Christmas spirit in Morocco. There were no Salvation Army bell ringers at every store to ignore, no Christmas songs being played on Muzak way too early in October while the Halloween decorations and candy was still on the shelves, and no anguishing over what was the most appropriate gift for the mailman. Without that extra stress, we had more time to adorn the house with decorations the girls made out of construction paper. Then we put up our pathetic Moroccan fake tree we bought the year before. It took all of an hour of festooning to make our massive, white-walled museum of a house look like a massive, white-walled museum of a house hosting a very white trash Christmas. Soundtrack by Kesha.

I was kinda bah-humbug on the whole Christmas thing anyway. I tried to enjoy the holiday but I did it mostly for the elements and Craig, who loved the magic of the season. I was just a skeptic and it pissed me off to watch how everyone treated their fellow man a bit kinder around mid-December then reverted back to their old ways mid-January. So I couldn't help but bring that unspirited version of myself to the Christmas celebration at the American ambassador's house.

Our almost Buddhist family went to the Jewish ambassador's house for a Christmas celebration where Santa handed out gifts to local Muslim kids who trampled the Christian kids to get them. That's how I saw it, anyway. Things started to turn around when we got a massive care package from my friend Deb in the states with every holiday goodie imaginable. That and leaving Morocco for our biggest adventure yet saved Christmas.

We left the northern most part of Africa and headed for the southern tip, South Africa, where our adventure started. That was also where the contrasts began. Morocco was an old monarchy. South Africa, a new democracy. A Moroccan winter was a South African summer. Morocco was predominantly Muslim; South Africa, mostly Christian. It was illegal to be homosexual in Morocco. South Africa was the only African country where being gay was legal. South African streets were clean and void of feral cats and astonishingly, drivers obeyed traffic laws. So driving was similar to the States except they drove on the wrong side of the road and sometimes the road was blocked by an elephant. Or an impala. Not to be confused with a Chevy Impala.

Our mission was to camp our way through South Africa, Botswana, Zambia and Zimbabwe with our good friends and traveling companions the Green family (Faith, Mark, Conor, Collin, Aidan, and Mark's parents Barb and Dale). We would brave the elements, the other elements, whining, lack of pillows and any privacy whatsoever for ten days. Just us against the wild beasts of Africa. Who would win? Team Man or Team Wild?

~

We traveled and camped through South Africa for two days before we reached Hazy View campground. We'd already seen an elephant with a curiously mutated tail shaped like a penis, bestowed our sympathies on a mangy lion close to death, coined the phrase awk-weird, and learned the camping routine. Then we'd wake up ridiculously early after another sleepless night listening to crazy monkey noises wondering exactly how crazy the monkeys got. Deposit the morning contribution in the toilet if there was one, to the earth if there wasn't, dismantle the tent, cook breakfast, clean up after breakfast, pack everything into the trailer, and load the van. Drive for a few hours before stopping to make lunch, clean up after lunch, get back in the car, drive to camp, arrive at camp, put the tent up, make dinner and clean up after dinner. Then the next morning it started all over again.

The GPS took us down a narrow dirt path through a lychee grove. I wasn't sure which was more ripe…the fruit on the trees or the smell emanating from a van full of sunscreened and mosquito repellent-drenched unshowered campers. But, I'm gonna guess Team Man won that battle. Our host told us we could eat as many lychees as we wanted, a dangerous invitation when you're traveling with friends and everyone had bubbling fruit gases in their guts. Friendships have been ruined by less.

We pitched our tents under the trees. We realized that was a really stupid place for a tent when we were pummeled by ripe fruit in the middle of the night. We had already been assaulted by offensive lychee farts during the day. It wasn't fair. We needed some kind of compensation for being stupid American gluttonous pigs. Something like a free meal. Yeah, a big buffet would make everything right. That was the Law of Similars: If too much food produced morbid symptoms, eat even more…or something like that. I didn't think it was a coincidence that the campground offered authentic South African food slow cooked over an open flame.

After we set up camp, we cooled down in a pool nature carved out of rock. Even though we'd rinsed off, we still were in desperate need of showering. Just like everything else, the shower was directly under a lychee tree. The toilets also followed the open-air-under-a-lychee-tree concept. Which was convenient. We could eat lychees and shit them out at the same time. No air freshener necessary, just the fresh South African breeze carrying the aroma of that nights' feast.

After lingering over a cocktail of coconut rum mixed with Sprite, the house specialty, we headed to dinner. A dinner cooked by someone else was bound to be fabulous. That's where we learned that dinner was chicken livers, chicken heads and chicken feet, also the house specialty. Bugs or chicken feet? I couldn't decide which I would like to eat less. Thank god we were eating with our hands because I wouldn't have known which fork to use for chicken heads. The beets, spinach and sweet potatoes were delicious. Even the kids ate them. Because chicken nuggets weren't an option.

The night ended with African dancing. The kind of dancing where a boob threatened to jiggle free of a much-too-small top worn by one of the local dancers. So no one blinked 'cause we didn't want to miss it. I must have looked like a skinny, white girl with rhythm because the dancers pulled me out to dance with them. And for just a short time while gyrating to the drumbeats and trying to keep up with some of the fittest women I've ever met, I was a part of something bigger, an international tribe of women. Until it was apparent I lacked two very big things: any knowledge of Sub-Saharan African dance and the inability to kick my leg up to my head. Oh, and boobs. I obviously didn't have those either.

The next day we crossed the border into Botswana and converted our South African rands into pula, the local currency. Our next campground didn't have lychees, dinner or cocktails. It was a dirt lot crawling with furry African caterpillars. No big deal. We could do dirt and a caterpillar wasn't a deadly snake. Unless it was a poisonous caterpillar.

We'd gotten really efficient at pitching tents by then, and good thing. Because the pelting monsoon rain came. We all huddled under the tin roof of a small outdoor kitchen with a fabulous bottle of red cooking up bangers and mash. Although that sounds perverted, it's sausage and potatoes, in American English. The blustery winds blew over our meticulously seasoned and reseasoned coleslaw twice. When the turbulent storm finally subsided right after dinner, it left a huge mud puddle shaped like Africa. Team Wild mocked us. We needed to prove our dominance so we played and danced in the mud puddles. We would not be defeated.

In the morning, we packed our damp belongings and headed north hoping for drier weather. Maybe my tribe had done an anti-rain dance. Because when we pulled into the next campground, Elephant Sands, we were greeted by sunny skies and an elephant. What were the chances an elephant would be right there? In Botswana, pretty damn good. Over 100,000 elephants live, trample and proudly parade through the country. Unlike all the other places we'd stayed, that site didn't have any gates to keep the wildlife out. Cool! We could be all one with nature and everything. Only later I remembered that the circle of life was quite natural, quite real, and quite scary.

It was one of the hottest days of the safari. Really hot. Africa hot. And dry, savanna dry. Perfect for drying out our trench feet, in theory, anyway. Setting up tents in the midday sun marinated us in sweat head to toe. After a brief dip in the pool that also doubled as a bath, we went on a game drive just down the road. Literally. Not even two miles from our unsecured campsite. That's when it started to sink in…there's no gate to protect us.

We were surrounded by ferocious animals. They were our neighbors, and we'd already made our presence known with our super noxious human stank. Any cheetah within seven miles could smell dinner. Human tartar. Not only that, the seven kids conveniently came in a cheetah fun size. You know, if the cheetah just felt like a snack and didn't want that post-Thanksgiving, I-ate-too-much-and-had-to-loosen-my-belt slumpy feeling.

Coincidentally, that was when we saw our first and only leopard on safari. It was sunning itself a couple city blocks from our tents. Of course, we weren't in the city, so there were no buildings, traffic or hot dog vendors to impede its stride. Which one was faster and more ferocious, the leopard or the cheetah? They could both kill us in less than a minute, so really, what did that even matter?

A day or so earlier, we'd discovered that the boomslang was an indigenous and very poisonous tree-dwelling snake. It was also Green family slang for a silent but deadly fart. I wasn't sure which was faster or more ferocious. They could both kill us in less than a minute so really, again, what did that even matter? But in the event that boomslangs were repelled by boomslangs, Team Man had us covered.

At this point during the game drive the driver pulled over and instructed us to get out of the jeep. What? Why would we do that? In Egypt that was the time we would baksheesh in order to be allowed back into the vehicle. But this was Botswana. It was just the part of the safari where we wandered the open savanna with a cold alcoholic beverage. A Savanna Dry, hard apple cider. Cause it was a great idea to slow your reaction time when you're being stalked by predators. But hell, it was happy hour. If I was going to be eaten alive by a crocodile, goddamn it, I wanted to be good and drunk.

When I started on my second bottle, I was totally fine with the kids standing on a tall termite mound, a virtual stage for all the animals in the savannah to get a glimpse and a whiff. Like a buffet line. Craig posed for a picture at the edge of crocodile-infested waters. Phew, so what if we saw a hippopotamus? Come on! I could totally take a hippo in a bar fight. If I didn't start crying because I'd been overcome with the sentimentality that could only be brought on by drinking too much. I mean, look how big the elements had gotten. Jade borrowed my red t-shirt soaked with my B.O. because we fit the same clothes now. The elements were going to leave home soon and then Craig and I all would be by ourselves, empty nesters. What would we talk about without the elements to complain about? Maybe I was getting ahead of myself.

We loaded back into the jeep and drove through some shallow but too deep for comfort brackish water. My buzz made everything that concerned me a bit less concerning. So what if we couldn't see the bottom of the water and didn't know what was swimming in it? So what if we got stuck? River stood up while we rode through the rough terrain without so much as a car door to break his fall. Not to worry. That child didn't have enough meat on his bones for any animal to be interested in eating him.

We stopped again for a photo opportunity at a baobab tree just like the huge artificial one at Disney's Animal Kingdom. Except I'm sure Disney would have charged me at least $10 for that Savanna Dry, River would have had to use a seatbelt and the campgrounds would have been gated with absolutely no chance of an animal attack because the animals would have all been animatronic. Real danger with real risk was way more fun.

We made it back to camp before dusk unscathed. We shared dinner with swarms of suicidal moths that flew themselves into our mouths and drowned themselves in our drinks kamikaze style. Warding off the minuscule threat of eating bugs distracted us from the monumental threat of being eaten. Before heading to my sleeping bag for the night, I ventured to the shower to wash off the fresh afternoon and evening sweat and dirt. Faith pointed out a massive African spider in the bathroom. While I'm not normally scared of spiders, this was the biggest, furriest one I'd ever seen. I didn't want to get into a shower stall naked with it without any means of defense. So chalk up a point for Team Wild.

Defeated, I headed to the tent I shared with Craig, stink and all. It was quiet and peaceful. At least for an hour or two. Then Craig unzipped the tent to investigate a curious noise. The stars lit up the silhouette of an elephant uprooting the bush next to us for a midnight snack. The trunk lifted the shrub to its mouth where it was methodically chewed into bite-size morsels. We watched him for several minutes until he sauntered off toward the watering hole. We drifted back to sleep for another hour or so before Craig opened the zipper for the second time.

"Where are you going?" I asked groggily.

"I gotta pee."

Cue a loud roar from an unknown distance.

"Did you hear that?" I asked. Hoping he'd say no. Even though I knew he wouldn't. Because you couldn't have not heard it.

"Yeah."

"What do you think that was?" Another stupid question I knew the answer to that one too.

"A lion."

Dammit, that's what I'd thought! "Can you see him?" I asked.

"Not if I'm not looking." He zipped the tent back up.

"So you're not going to go pee, then?" I asked.

"Not right now, no."

"Come here and smell my armpit." I wanted to determine our danger level.

"I don't need to. I can smell you from here."

"You, too!" I was quick to return the compliment.

"I think I heard Mark's parents get out of their tent to pee!" Craig said worried.

"What do we do? Do we go after them? Wait. Are they smellier than us?"

"They'll be OK. Mark's mom is pretty scrappy. She could take a lion."

"She's all of five foot one. Maybe!"

"Have you seen her take Mark out in a verbal smackdown? Do you remember what she said about waiting for him in the rain when he was in track in high school only to watch your kid come in last?" he asked.

"That was hilarious! OK, yeah, you're right. She could totally take the lion."

So that's when we fed Grandma and Grandpa Green to the lions. We weren't proud of it. In fact, it was the second time I was filled with shame for ignoring my moral obligation to say and do the right thing in Africa. Don't worry, grandma and grandpa were completely unharmed. Craig and I confessed the next day. So it all turned out for the best. Plus they got to pee and slept comfortably the rest of the night. Well, mildly less uncomfortably in a sleeping bag on the hard ground on top of a swarm of millipedes.

~

When we crossed from Botswana into Zambia on the ferry, we instantly became millionaires. Zambia's currency, kwatcha, was so worthless there were 5,000 to every U.S. dollar. Craig degraded it even further by nicknaming it crotch-ya. Even though we were millionaires, our cash wouldn't get us very far. When we arrived in Livingstone early that afternoon, we heard there'd been an accident. A girl had bungee jumped off the bridge that connected Zambia to Zimbabwe and the cord broke. The rumor was vague and void of details, so we assumed she'd died.

Back in Morocco, we learned that a twenty-two-year-old Australian woman's bungee cord broke and she plunged into the crocodile-infested waters. Despite some extensive bruising, she was relatively unscathed. As with all things these days, it was caught on video and in no time it had been broadcast all over the world.

The next day, we headed to Victoria Falls and saw the bridge where the accident had occurred. I grew up just outside Niagara Falls, which I'd assumed was the biggest waterfall in the world. It's only ranked number three. But it's the number one wonder of the world that has been ruined by the world's worst tourist attractions. It's infested with casinos and cheesy wax museums on the Canadian side. The American side is far worse, infested with drugs and dilapidated housing.

Guess which waterfall ranks the second biggest in the world? Yup. Victoria Falls. The largest is Iguazu Falls in Argentina, if you must know. I put it on my travel list. After growing up near the glitz and subsequent disappointment of a tourist attraction that was more about cocaine, gambling, and a life-size Liberace made out of wax, I was skeptical that this one would be similarly adulterated. But I was delightfully surprised to be greeted by a hand-painted and charmingly misspelled sign stating *Entrence Victoria Falls*. Complete with freely roaming monkeys to guard the perimeter. Nature as nature intended it to be. Wild.

It was so simple and natural there weren't even guard rails or signs to keep stupid people from doing stupid things. Like standing on the rocks right next to the rapids at the top of the falls where the water plummeted off the precipice. Which was exactly where Craig headed with the elements and some of the Green kids too. It all would have been fine if those kids had just been secured by a bungee cord or something. But they weren't, so I reeled them back in.

We ended up on the bridge where the bungee incident had occurred less than 24 hours earlier. The accident hadn't slowed business at all. Ember begged me to let her jump. She was six. Even if she'd been thirty-six, I still would have clutched her to my chest until she'd promised never to do that or get a tramp stamp. The parking lot was flooded with vendors selling all kinds of hand crafted trinkets including a funky straw zebra I really wanted but was too cheap to pay $40 for. I could've gotten it cheaper if I'd bought it at World Market, for god's sake. Surely Pier One would have it too. But they'd charge $200, which could feed a Zambian family for a year but it wouldn't because it would feed corporate greed instead.

## JUST A HOUSEWIFE

We left Zambia and started our long journey home. First we'd need to cross into Zimbabwe and drive to the airport. We had carefully reserved just enough cash for the visas we needed. Crazy, screwed up, currency-less Zimbabwe where 90% of its people are literate, which is unheard of in Africa. Equally unheard of, 95% of its people are underemployed.

We get on the bus that takes us across the border. Passing the wild monkeys and women balancing baskets, duffel bags and their extended families on their heads. We fill out the immigration card on the bus. There's one question that always confounds me on official documents: Occupation. What do I do, anyway? Who am I? I haven't yet called myself a writer because I've never earned any money for that. So after a mini identity crisis, I settle on mother.

We file off the bus and into the immigration office for our visas. Our foreignness bumps us straight to the front of the line. Screwing over the locals and consuming me with white guilt. The officer processes the kids first. Which throughout Africa involves some very loud stamping of passports, visas and miscellaneous papers. When he gets to my passport and the immigration form, he mumbles, laughs, scratches out *mother* and inserts *housewife*. Instantaneously I'm demeaned and approved for entry. Housewife? I am not, nor have I ever been, married to my house.

Our friends the Greens are next in line. Faith is the editor of the embassy newsletter. Turns out that anything related to journalism garners another form. One that says that you will not take pictures of or write anything about Zimbabwe. Which she signed in exchange for her visa. I don't have to do that. I'm just a housewife.

We used the last of our cash on the visas. We ask the driver if we had enough time to stop at the market and still make it to the airport in time. We have about twenty minutes to spare. Of course, we're broke and they don't take credit cards in shanty towns. What we do have are six unwashed bath towels we've used for showering and at the pools for the last two weeks. They're disgustingly filthy. Plus, I brought our old threadbare towels on safari and at this point, funky does not begin to describe their stench. So I bundle all our towels in my arms.

I am a terrible bargainer. I like set prices where I can simply decide if I want to pay that price or not. But I can't do that because all I have is towels. Which in a way makes this all easier. I know you're wondering who would want those putrid towels. Here, everyone does. All the vendors are salivating over my towels and trying to get me to trade them for souvenirs. And they'll do almost anything.

I'm looking for one thing. Remember that zebra I didn't get in Zambia? I have less than twenty minutes to find it and more than forty vendors to bargain with. Can it be done? Hell, yes! Who knew I'm the freaking queen of skanky towel trading? Next time when I get a visa form and they ask for occupation I'm going to write *skanky towel trader* in that box.

For six towels I scored not one but two zebras, a small wooden elephant, a decorative plate, an urn, bracelets for Jade and Ember, a necklace for Sky and a small trinket for River.

You know what? If I was a writer, I couldn't have told you this story at all. So I just got a new appreciation for being a housewife. And I'm starting to think this is a pretty sweet gig. My house doesn't care how much time I spend in it. It doesn't care if I roller skate through it. Or if I completely neglect and don't clean it. Or appreciate it. And most of all? I can write anything, anytime, anywhere and I don't have to answer to anyone. So, I kinda like being just a housewife. I don't need anyone to validate who or what I am, especially with a stupid loud official stamp!

# Chapter 17

# Homesick

On the last day of every vacation when I should be enjoying the final moments of wherever I am, I can't. My mind wanders home to all the crap I need to do when I get there. Several loads of laundry, stocking the fridge with food, paying the bills, and all the other thankless errands made ever more complex by living in a foreign country. The more I try to stop obsessing about these stupid little things, the more I needlessly worry about them. They would either get done or they wouldn't. The world would continue to spin. It always did.

We had six more months in Morocco and I was trying not to check out mentally before we left. We started to make plans to move back home, chose dates, talked to moving companies, and finalized arrangements for our house. Which meant I was thinking more about Colorado every day. How much I'd missed my friends and the everyday details of their lives. About my meager, cozy Colorado house that didn't have a ginormous gate around it. I missed the mountains. I missed roller derby. I missed English. And god knew, I missed baby spinach. Though I wasn't going to dwell on that, even though I did.

The truth was that no one in the States could possibly understand how much I'd miss the absurdity that is Morocco. I'd miss the ASS and Sara and the everyday details of their lives. The countless calamities I'd circumvent. We wouldn't be fifteen minutes, two surfboards, four boogie boards, six towels, loads of sunscreen, a blanket, an umbrella and a packed lunch from the beach. 'Cause that was just so convenient. I would miss not understanding anything at my belly dance class. And driving without rules. What about Barrack, my favorite parking guy? He'd think I had forgotten all about him.

It was even more than that. I would miss the complicated simplicity that is Morocco. The way everything was pared down to basics. We either needed something for survival or we didn't. Anything and anyone unnecessary got cut. And, for the most part, we hadn't missed anything. We'd had everything we'd needed. We had it all along. All we needed was to be together, supporting each other or smacking the mosquitos off each other, no matter where in the world we were.

And to think that at the beginning of this journey I was willing to jeopardize the very thing that was most important to me, my family. This adventure wasn't about showing the kids the world and making them grateful for what they had after all. This was about me realizing I'd held the world in my hands the whole time. All I needed to do was to have the strength to see things for what they really were. Perfectly imperfect. And to think I was on the brink of starting my own familial World War III when we arrived in Morocco, deluded that divorce might be the answer to the inner peace I sought. When it was merely acceptance of all my misgivings all along.

Morocco turned out to be a solo journey into my core and I'd brought my favorite people in the world along for the ride. I could have stayed there indefinitely, putting off re-entering the real world a while longer basking in a serenely crowded solitude, but the elements were anxious to get back to the States. Positive they'd missed so much having been away for so long. Truth is, none of us had.

I was homesick. Despite being unsure where exactly home was anymore. For most of my adult life, I'd been homeless. While Craig was in the Army, we'd moved every couple of years. I learned not to establish roots or get too close or too dependent on anyone or anything, the way frequent movers do. Although on the outside I might have looked cool, confident and independent, I secretly wanted all those things a transient lifestyle made so difficult. Friends that all lived in the same city as me. And a real place to call home.

Answering the question, "So where are you from?" at a party was complex. Did they mean where I was born? Where I grew up? Where I went to college? Bachelors or Masters? Where I met my husband? The favorite place I've ever lived? Or the last place I moved from?

We moved to Colorado on a whim. The month before Craig had finished his Army contract, after having sold his soul in exchange for a paid ride through medical school, we had to choose where to settle down. The government was reluctantly ready to cut us loose and ship our stuff there. Uncle Sam, in all its omniscience, had always chosen for us. The freedom to choose was stifling for a split second until it was enticingly liberating. We were free to do anything we damn well pleased. Our back up plan which was now as old as the tearing down of the Berlin wall, was that we'd end up in Orlando where the largest chunk of Craig's family congregated. Until it came time to choose.

I love many people who live in Florida. The thing is, I hate Florida itself. Sure, the beaches are nice. But, who can afford to live on the beach? Even if you could, you'd live in a modest sea-level bungalow with sky high homeowner's insurance right on hurricane highway. I know this after four years of living in sweltering Miami constantly being called Maria. We were there in our tiny apartment in North Miami beach where we were the youngest people by at least a 40 year age gap, when Hurricane Andrew hit. Taking down the huge tree in the courtyard that obscured our perverted old neighbors from looking into our bedroom window.

Then I did what I do with all the important decisions in my life. I didn't research like a practical person; I daydreamed. And I was extremely subtle and eloquent when I broached the topic with Craig.

"I really hate Florida. I don't want to live there," I said. 'Cause I'm tactful like that.

Craig, as usual, patiently listened and considered what I had to say.

"The only reason we'd move there is for your family," I said. "We've lived all over and see them anyway. It's kinda like they stalk us. Plus, the army will pay. And I think we both know they need to repay us!"

"So, what do you want to do?" he asked. Because he knew I had a point. (And that I was right.)

"I want to move somewhere that has the life we want to live. Somewhere you can be outside most of the year without being drenched and marinated in your own sweat. Without strip malls filled with bail bond places, where we don't need air conditioning and there aren't strip joints on every corner...." Pause for drama. "Like Colorado."

After careful consideration, Craig loved the idea. Then he spent countless hours on the internet researching home prices, schools, taxes, air quality, and how fluoridated the water was. When he was done, he then spent even more time asking countless friends, acquaintances, coworkers and patients what they thought about Colorado. The culmination of my five-second daydream and Craig's all-consuming quest was that we ended up in Colorado Springs without a job or any prospects, without knowing a soul with three hungry mouths to feed along with two big ones with a penchant for more expensive organic, gourmet ingredients.

It didn't take long to figure out that we were anomalies in that tight little town. We didn't go to the Air Force Academy, train at the Olympic Training Center, we didn't know what a fourteener was and we didn't know what the hell Focus on the Family focused on. They are an intensely myopic mainstream pro-Jesus organization, in case you didn't know. We didn't own mountain bikes, ski, or do triathlons in really tight, way-too-much-information biking shorts. We didn't have friends, but we were surrounded by trees, mountains, fresh air and the occasional bear, mountain lion, rattlesnake, waft of pot smoke and each other. Maybe one day we'd fit in but we hoped we never would. Maybe we could find other likeminded misfits we could befriend. Although that seemed unlikely.

I found them at the elements' new school, a group of kindergarten moms I stalked for several months. Having known each other for years, they were a tight-knit group of smart, outspoken, irreverent and most important, funny women. But, they didn't appear to be taking applications.

I wanted in. I tried to be a considerate, inconspicuous stalker. I'd show up early for drop off and linger after pickup trying to make casual conversation with my targets while trying not to appear creepy like I knew their daily schedule and where they lived and that they wore that same pair of pants on Monday, although I did. It went on this way for months. Me pretending to be normal and sociable. Finally, I wore them down with my sheer determination that we would be friends. Not by threatening them that I'd teepee their houses every night, although I would have stooped to that. They invited me to lunch for Indian food. There was no greater sign of having made a new friend than a lunch invitation for ethnic food. That's how I came upon my best and closest friends—happenstance with some indiscriminate mild to moderate stalking.

Most of us are in or around our forties now. By this point in life, we've had the fun that the twenties brought, the career of our thirties, we might have had some kids unless certain people decided dogs were better and more loyal companions that didn't need a clothing allowance. Either way, by the time anyone reaches this pre-mid-life point, you have a pretty good idea what you want out of life. Although you might just be too damn busy with so many obligations and commitments to have any time left to devote to getting it. Whatever it is for you. Unless you go temporarily crazy and get a bit sidetracked for a while, which also frequently happens at this age.

The forties, especially if you're married raising children, are the most stressful and statistically least happy years of life. It's true. I read it in a human development book somewhere along the line. Which makes it that much more important to surround yourself with people you love and can commiserate with, preferably over a glass of red or a shot of tequila, depending on the day.

In Colorado, one of my best friends got divorced the year after her brother committed suicide. Another friend lost his job right after he discovered the son he'd sent off to college had developed a heroin addiction. Another friend was slowly losing a parent to Alzheimer's, memory by memory. The gym teacher's daughter was in a horrific skiing accident. After clinging to life for months in intensive care, she emerged permanently disabled. Then there was the neighborhood schoolboy who suffered brain damage when he was hit by a teenager drag racing through the streets, two of his siblings were killed. Facebook brought even more bad news and tragedy, extending the circle of depressing current events back to the people we'd known in high school.

Grief and loss were global. In Morocco it arrived with a phone call. Bad news always starts with a ringing telephone. Jenny's dad was sick. Just three weeks earlier she'd gotten another call when one of her closest friends died from cancer. Her family feared the c-word but everyone was hopeful, so no one said it out loud. The tests confirmed that it was the fastest, deadliest kind, pancreatic cancer. He didn't have much time left and she was a world away tying to grasp the brutal reality of it.

My phone call had come twelve years earlier, soon after my thirtieth birthday. I'd been living in Oklahoma and had gone back to school to get a Masters in Psychology so I could become a therapist, of all things, when mom told me she'd started forgetting things. I didn't think much of it at first. Until she was diagnosed with brain cancer. The quickest and most deadly kind. I moved back in with my parents and spent the last two months of her life taking care of her. Time that I treasure. Holding her hand, cooking her meals and kissing her goodnight just like she'd done for me when I'd been little.

They say time heals all wounds but that's bullshit. Wounds scab and crust. They're itchy and against our better judgment, we scratch them. With time that scab become a scar that will never go away. Grief is a solitary, lonely place. You can't bypass it or control it. Long after the casseroles and sympathy cards disappear, the scars are still there. Testaments to arduous pilgrimage. Leaving you the same yet completely transformed forever.

Your friends pull you back into the land of the living. They remind you not to waste the precious time you have left. Reminding you love is worth the heartbreak over and over again and that laughter is worth peeing your pants for.

## REINTEGRATION

We were moving back to the States in a matter of months. And it occurred to me I had become a bit Moroccanized. To reintegrate into American culture, I needed to start polishing myself and I needed to start now.

Teeth. Americans are obsessed with perfect teeth. They must be brushed, flossed and straight. Oh yeah, and white. Really, really white. Which is why I ordered some white strips from A-mer-i-kah. Because no one sells that crap here. Moroccans are simply grateful to have teeth that haven't rotted out from drinking uber-sugary, teeth-staining Moroccan mint tea.

Since I'm American, being grateful for what I have isn't enough. The only thing between me and perfect Chiclet teeth is ten days of putting a plastic strip laden with a non-toxic, enamel safe gel that I should keep out of reach of children in my mouth. That makes me feel tingly inside...inside my mouth at least. Not in a good way, either. But I think we all know the success of an American is judged by how well his or her teeth glow in the dark. You can get catapulted to Snooki status if they contrast with your spray tan. I don't know why you'd want to, though.

TV. I've never been one to watch sports, soap operas or reality shows. Which automatically makes me un-American. I used to watch my fair share of news magazines and HGTV. Since we don't have TV in Morocco, we rely on other means of entertainment. Namely illegal bootleg DVDs bought from the shady guy at the medina or illegal copies given to us by friends. That's how we came upon the TV series *How I Met Your Mother*. I'd never seen it before because seriously, isn't that one of the stupidest titles ever? But with nothing else to do, we put it in and became completely addicted. Now we'll be able to catch all those *How I Met Your Mother* references when we return. We might even be caught up on the whole series by the time we get home. We're going to be so American culture literate.

Social Graces. Soon after we moved to Morocco, I dispensed with all unnecessary social graces. So I could make room in my brain for all that French and Darija I was going to learn that I never did. Anyway, I've lost that instinctive American reaction to bless someone when they sneeze. Blessing someone here would require a lengthy explanation as to why we would bless people yet deny Americans with preexisting conditions health insurance. Which must be exactly why we bless people.

Not only that but I've gotten far more lax about other social graces. Like refraining from picking my nose in the car. 'Cause there's no shame in it here. After all, everyone else does it. I imagine this is the kind of thing that self-corrects after that first humiliating nose pick witnessed through a car window back in the States where we openly mock such gross necessities.

Music. I have come to truly appreciate Arabic music and the fact that if the lyrics are completely stupid and nonsensical like the song *Abracadabra* by Steve Miller, I am blissfully unaware. Branching out musically is a big deal for me. I don't like country, nor western. I don't like techno or dance. I hate rap. I abhor pop.

We do get non-Arabic music here. We get frap, French crap. Have you heard French rap? It's a language that's not conducive to sounding angry or gangsta. Of course we get pop. Even though most songs are in English, they're often so bad I assume they were written by someone for whom English is a second language. Often they don't make sense. Just the other day, I heard that *We Speak No Americano* song. What the hell is that crap? And why do they play that shit incessantly on the radio? I didn't realize it was an international hit, kinda like *International Love*, but worse.

Personal Hygiene. Americans are very sensual. And we like it everywhere. In our car. At home.

No. I spelled that wrong, I mean scentual. Everything must have a scent. Starting with our bodies. And it needs to be pleasant, like baby powder fresh or mountain fresh. Emphasis on the fresh. Which probably means I should start using deodorant again. Before I do that, I should probably start shaving my armpits again. I can't decide which of those things Americans would find more repulsive...hairy pits or stinky pits. Therefore I should do both. Sometime. Before June.

Queuing Up. I used to know how to stand in a line. I also used to know the rules of the road and who had the right of way. Since I don't use any of those social pleasantries here, I've forgotten them. I could probably stand in a line without elbowing because I only do that in self-defense. No full-blooded American will allow anyone to cut in line so it wouldn't even get that far.

But I don't know if I can go back to following road rules again. Honestly, I was never good at it. I won't get a ticket in Morocco because I've learned not to stop for the cop. But I'm wondering how long it'll be before I get pulled over in the States. And how long it will take for him to catch up with me.

Things are looking a bit bleak for a seamless reentry. At least I'll have white teeth. Except that Ember opened the white strips and pasted them to the sides of the sink. So I might not even have that. But, I do have a very white sink.

# Chapter 18

# Democratic Non-secular Soul Searching

It was left at a friend's doorstep with a note. It was too heavy and cumbersome for one person to move, so it had to be opened where it lay. A chill caught the air as its contents were revealed. A blood bath of liquescent ice surrounded the intact but mortally wounded victim. Boar. The other, other white meat.

The corpse needed to be kept cold but it would have to be hacked into smaller pieces to fit in the refrigerator. They took it to the only place equipped for the job, a joint where not being *halal* wasn't a problem. The pork lady. Though she had all the tools for the job, apparently health codes prevented her from cutting up a wild boar of unknown origins. Strangely, no health codes prevented one from selling and eating a fly-ridden goat head that hung outside all day in August sun down the medina way.

The boar had been on ice for two days. Something had to be done stat. But who would have the tools to do such a job? The gardener. I didn't ask how it was done. Although I imagine a hoe was involved. However, I dared not ask. All I know was that I wasn't an accessory to the brutality and hacking. And I got my piece from the massacre. The whole gang came over on Valentine's Day to devour it.

Well, not the whole gang. We had to exclude Muslims. And Mormons. Not in a religious discrimination kinda way, but in a heathen, carnal pork doused in red wine kinda way. Nothing personal. Even though food segregated people there sometimes, it wasn't nearly like it is in the States. Moroccans don't suffer food allergies the way Americans do . There was no peanut-free table at my kids' school because no one was going to blow up like a helium balloon and die from a peanut butter cookie. I'd never met a Moroccan vegan. No restaurant catered to the Paleo diet because that would exclude the national dish, couscous.

So, with the exception of serving a drunk boar, not to be confused with a drunk bore, which we'd also experienced, it was much easier to have a dinner party there. I didn't have to figure out how to make something wheat-less, meat-less, cheese-less, sugarless, nut, fat and alcohol-free taste good.

No, my biggest food conundrum was feeding Jenny, who had the weird psychological food issues of a toddler. She didn't like her food touching. Countless textures were repugnant to her and she didn't like anything spicy. She was the queen of bland and frequently made gagging noises at the dinner table without shame. She was more challenging to feed than the elements. Other than the Jenny factor, it was easier to share a meal with friends in Morocco. Thank god, because it was hard to go out to dinner, especially with kids, because restaurants don't even open for dinner until 8:00 p.m. And that was the American equivalent of going to Golden Corral at 4:30 for the early bird special. Although the meals were much longer and there weren't any heating lamps.

Going out to dinner was too long, late and cumbersome for American standards. Plus, there's only so much Moroccan chicken tagine with olives one could endure anyway. Unless we were traveling, we ate at home. With the less than appetizing choices with even less appetizing smells available at the grocery store.

Like lamb. Sinewy, piquant, ubiquitous lamb. It didn't matter how you prepared it, it would still be lamby and I don't mean that in a good way. *Halal* beef was less tender, and we ate more than our fair share of boring chicken. I was constantly on the lookout for anything new and exciting. I was ecstatic when I found duck and cooked it for the first time in an orange sauce with a hint of ginger. Then I made duck with prunes. And duck with pears. The elements didn't give a duck for any of it. They also don't like ostrich steak in a shallot red wine glaze. You can take the kids out of America but you can't take away their love of cheap, crap, processed non-foods like chicken nuggets…which we could get there. Thanks, McDonald's, for exporting America's food issues worldwide so almost everyone everywhere has a chance at experiencing type 2 diabetes.

Food has always been the great common denominator. All humans need it to survive. Not everyone has enough of it though. It's political. Wars have started over food or rather the lack of it. And all of us have our own personal battles with food. Some hoard, others deny, many gorge or binge. Then there are the pretentious, who preach that they alone can claim to speak the gospel of food. Which might not be a food at all but a superfood nutritional supplement they're selling through Amway. Then of course there's the religious aspects of food. Eating fish on Fridays, being vegetarian and of course not eating pork. But do any of these bring us closer to god? Or is that just drinking wine? I guess none of us know for sure until we're dead.

I wanted to be an example for the elements. Cooking for them was so important to me. I wanted them to grow up with a balanced view of food, to be healthy but not judgmental about other people's food choices. I wanted them to embrace food and fill their bellies until their spirit was stuffed preferably with a lot of vitamins and minerals and a shit ton of fiber. I'm pretty sure that's where the term soul food originated. But what the hell do I know?

~

We were invited to a celebration at the Embassy. Our friend Doug was retiring from the Air Force. It was an idyllic sunny day filled with reflection, possibilities and new beginnings. The festivities continued into the balmy summer evening. We celebrated the way Americans do by barbecuing hamburgers and hot dogs and bringing dishes to share. We swigged back some drinks in toast, which resulted in some ending up toasted.

At the end of the evening, I dragged the elements away from playing volleyball on the lawn in the dark. My bubbling bliss had come from a full belly and night full of friendship and fun. Unless that was a bubbling gas or my buzz. Anyway, when I crawled into bed that night, I was at peace with the world.

Weeks later, I was over at Faith's house chitchatting and helping her in the kitchen. That's when I saw a familiar package. For some reason, I picked it up and browsed the label. "Oh, shit!"

Then I replayed the events of the party for Faith, who'd been out of town that evening. I skipped directly to the moment where it had all gone wrong. My transgression. I'd been at the food table trying to balance another scoop of potato salad on top of an already heaping flimsy paper plate. M (an unnamed bubble person) asked about the pepperoni in the pasta salad I'd made. "No worries, it's turkey pepperoni", I said.

Now, reading the label, I was wrong. It was pork. I'd fed pork to a Muslim. Who better to guide me in my quest to absolve myself of this sin than Faith? I mean, her name is Faith. If anyone had the answer, she would.

"What the hell do I do now?" I asked.

"Don't do anything," she advised.

"Would Hail Mary's help? Wait. I don't even think I remember how it goes. Does the unknowing pork eater go to hell? Or do I, the non-malicious pork perpetrator? Wait. Is hell like an office cubicle with piped in Muzak?"

"You don't even know if M ate it or not. J (another nameless expat) put pork in her Thanksgiving stuffing and knowingly fed it to Moroccans who are Muslim. She used to live in the big abandoned house down the street that used to be a brothel. She said men rang the doorbell at all times of the night a whole year after it was closed down."

"Did they come for her pork stuffing or to pork her? At least she'll be in the hell line ahead of me. The express lane." I hoped she would make those bacon-wrapped dates I've heard were her specialty. Then we could make it like a hell tailgating party. That's when I saw myself for the culturally insensitive person I was despite all my delusions to the contrary.

I only hope I haven't passed my depravity on to the elements. They have learned important life lessons like how to bargain for a pocketknife in the medina. Although, they got that from Craig. They also know that that knife was made by Chinese slave children with lead paint. And that China sold counterfeit goods, manipulated its currency and stole America's jobs. They got that from me. A team effort to keep things real. Real depressing, like it is in the real world.

Craig and I were good together like that. We'd always had similar views on the world; we just navigated through it differently. He traveled with a map and a compass. I felt my way through enabled only with a keen sense of smell. Together we've made some good decisions for the right reasons with only slightly corrupted morals most of the time.

More than anything, we want the elements to think for themselves and be who they truly are no matter what their religion, sexual orientation, political affiliation or if they choose to become gluten-free-paleo-vegans. Obviously that last one would be really hard. But, I'm sure they could do it if they set their minds to it.

~

When we told the elements Hillary Clinton was coming to Rabat and that we were going to go hear her speak, they were excited. I was excited they knew who she was. It was like a social studies pop quiz and they all aced it. I was setting the foundation for a deep love of politics and getting involved. I was sure of it. Although, deep down inside, I knew they only wanted to see the swarming security suited up complete with cool earpieces packing really cool pieces in a covert armpit holster. I still took it as them taking an interest in the world around them. Even if it was the world of espionage that intrigued them.

Hillary was in town to break ground on the new U.S. embassy, which was across the street from the King's palace. Coincidence? I think not. Anyway, what's weird was that he was out of town during her visit. The newly elected prime minister met with her instead, whatever his name was. It was too taxing to remember it or what he did even though that list wasn't very long.

I wonder what they talked about if they got together behind closed doors. She might have whispered something like, "Dude, do you realize you only got the crap powers? Really, dude, the King is still the leader of the military *and* the religious leader *and* can veto anything you do. You know you're a tool, right?"

Or maybe she said, "So I noticed there's only one token woman in your ministry. And she's the head of Women, Family and Social Development which, come on, we all know has a small budget and weak influence. That's a condescending slap in the face to women everywhere! Why don't you just say a woman's place is pregnant, barefoot and in the kitchen. Say it to my face!"

Or maybe it was, "What's your name again?"

Unless they just gossiped about the King the whole time.

Despite the open worldliness we were trying to instill in the elements, I'd become a bit more skeptical about the world. Unless I'd always been a skeptic wary of people's true intentions.

## PARANOID

I've thought about writing this post for a long time. I shelved the idea after The King and I post. At the time, I thought a post about being paranoid might be misconstrued as being related to that. Which it's not. Then I thought only people living in Morocco would truly understand what I have to say here. And then I worried about how many things I really, really want to say but for many reasons, like security, can't. Once I edited, would there be anything left? Which makes me sound certifiable and narcissistic but I just don't care anymore.

I've mentioned before how visible foreigners are here. Extremely. And that the minivan with its yellow diplomat plate sets me apart from all the small cars, mopeds and donkey carts on the road and declares I'm an American. What's the big deal, right? When you live overseas, the big deal is that not everyone likes Americans. Which is why my dad's advice for my first solo foreign adventure at eighteen was, "If anyone asks, tell them you're Canadian." Which of course is a half-truth. He was right...everyone likes a Canadian; they just don't respect them.

Then there's home security. Not homeland security but the actual security features of my house. My street has Moroccan guards around the clock (the general of the Moroccan army also lives on my street). Someone's always watching and knows when I leave my house, when I come home, when we go on vacation, when my husband is out of town, and when I yell at my kids. Again, so what?

It's common knowledge that the guards can earn even more money selling this common knowledge. So, the man in his late twenties or early thirties loitering on the corner with a notebook isn't a shorthand student on a lunch break. The house next door is under construction. And the twelve construction workers who live there (yes, they live in the house they're building) also know when I come, when I go, when we're on vacation, when my husband is out of town, and when I'm yelling at my kids.

Then there's the nine-foot wall around my house that doesn't make me feel safe at all. Just two weeks ago an American family in our area was robbed while they were sleeping with their three children upstairs. They also had a nine-foot wall, 24/7 neighborhood security guards, and an alarm system. What did the thieves steal? Their American passports. The guard probably got paid enough that he helped boost the thieves over the gate. Criminal justice Moroccan style.

These things happen in the States too. I know that. I do. But these kinds of things happen more frequently here. And they're scarier because the familiar American justice system isn't what we have to deal with if things go wrong.

I was at a friend's house when a guy she didn't know appeared at her door. He told her to tell the Loerzels that our car was unlocked. The thing is, I didn't know the person. And this wasn't the first time that had happened. One time I was at a park and someone came right up to me and said, "Marie, you need to lock your car."

Making friends was another issue I'd been extremely cautious about. Because we live among the embassy's transient, fast-paced but often abbreviated friend-making circuit. It makes me wonder if potential friends are interested in me or my Americanism. If these people are American, I'm wondering if they're interested in me or because I speak English and breathe. I've also learned to be suspicious about what people claim they do for a living. And whether they're befriending me for some work-related reason, if you know what I mean. Although that would be dumb because I'm unemployed and can't get anywhere in my own career, let alone yours.

Which transitions into the next part, my blog. I don't know who reads it. Unless you tell me you do. So there's a whole group of people out there who know things about me and my family even though I don't know them. Most people in Rabat don't know or care that I write a blog. Then there's the other fraction of a percentage. I am far more private and shy than I might seem in print. So if I'm in the grocery store and you're looking at me a little too long, I assume you're staring at the huge zit on my chin or I have a protruding booger or something. Not that you might be wondering where you might have seen me before.

Now, you might think I'm crazy, self-important and over exaggerating. If so, I know you're not an expat in Morocco. Because everyone here is a bit paranoid, even the King. A couple of months ago some of his former employees wrote an unflattering tell-all book called *The Predator King*. Guess who doesn't want you to read it? Because for some reason I can't find it anywhere. I hear you can buy a bootleg French copy in the medina. Just make sure no one's following you if you decide to get one and painstakingly Google translate it into English line by line.

# Chapter 19

## Talkin' Turkey

While some people like to waste time on video games, TV and playing Bejeweled Blitz, I liked to spend hours on Facebook. Reading status updates that bragged about happy, fulfilled lives perfectly lived complete with gorgeous photos to prove it so I could feel like crap about mine. Until I read a link on someone's wall that the more time you spend on Facebook, the more depressed you feel.

That's when I started to limit my exposure and decrease my online interactions that made me feel hollow and even more flawed and worthless than I already was. I traded in the fantasies that everyone's life was happier than mine for the notion that my life was happier when I travelled more. Then I spent hours searching vacation destinations and almost singlehandedly froze Expedia.com by searching several travel itineraries expeditiously. That's how I discovered a great deal, an authentically great deal this time, to Istanbul over spring break.

I'd never given Turkey a thought, I mean really? Who does? But I went ahead and bought the tickets without a second thought. It was only later, when I researched the country, that I found out all kinds of weird and unusual facts about it.

Like the Dutch originally got their tulips from Turkey. Talk about false advertising! Those sneaky Dutch!

And in the middle ages, Turkey had over 1,400 public toilets while none of the palaces in France had them. Oh, toilet paper wasn't invented until the mid-1800's. Ewww.

Istanbul boasts the third oldest subway in the world, though it's only on one street. (Not the restaurant chain, just for clarification.)

Turkey introduced coffee to Europe. That must be why Starbucks now owns Europe. Or at least some of its best real estate.

Oil wrestling has been a sport there since 1361. Before you imagine hot women in bikinis, it was a male sport. 'Cause I know where you were going with that train of thought.

It's one of the few countries that is agriculturally self-sufficient. Isn't that nuts? Which is a major export for them too, by the way.

95% of people there believe there is a god, while 99% of people identify themselves as Muslim. I'm not real good at math and I don't know a lot about Islam but that doesn't quite add up, does it?

Noah's ark landed here. No kidding! But it might have just been for a potty stop.

Istanbul is the only city to span two continents. What a fat ass!

When I bought the tickets I'd thought the whole Turkey gig was a consolation prize. Post Turkey cyberstalking, I thought we'd hit the jackpot.

~

The short plane ride was drudgery. No movie. No headphones. Only a gulp of a free high fructose corn syrup rich drink, a worthless inflight magazine and endless time for obsessions to take over. I ruminated on my insecurities while the elements dwelled on the new iPod Jade had bought with her own money and packed in her carryon. It seemed like a natural reward for having good grades and saving money. Forgetting that the natural consequence for providing kids with valuable lessons was they don't come easy, especially while traveling. It was the longest short flight we'd ever taken.

We'd connected at the Madrid airport during our trip to Egypt. The kids remembered it well. Not Madrid but the broken gum ball machine that gives out free cavity pullers if they jiggled the handle just right. We scored some Spanish gum at the newsstand. Where our boys scored a peek at a topless magazine cover placed precariously at their eye level.

The flight served dinner. An indecipherable slab that looked like Spam was the entree. It required a placard declaring it wasn't pork. Even though we couldn't figure out what it was. Luckily, wine was free on European airlines because they were civilized like that. At least there was some free perk for each of us to enjoy about international travel. Boobs, gum and wine. Something for everyone.

We arrived at midnight on the European side of the city. The ATM in front of the visa desk dispensed Euros. Weird, because Turkey's currency was the Lira. Turks must have been as confused as the rest of the world over whether they were in the European Union or not. On all of our travels we'd learned that nothing was what it seemed. Not a destination, a family or a marriage. The only constants were the forces constantly at work changing everything we thought we already knew.

We gave our driver the address of our apartment on the Asian side of the city. He had no idea where it was. So I pulled out my papers to look for the phone number of Karol, the guy who owned the apartment we'd rented. Turns out I hadn't brought it. The driver called someone presumably to ask directions, which was done by yelling into the phone. This is the part of the world where decibels rule. Before I moved to Morocco, my quiet timidity had always been my Achilles heel. After two years in Morocco, I finally stopped taking other peoples rudeness personally. And no longer apologized when some asshole rammed their shopping cart into me. My polite Canadianess had only exacerbated my codependency over the years. I was determined not to be incurably puerile anymore.

We took in the city lit by glistening street lamps. It was past midnight and kids were still out playing on the sidewalks. A woman in a headscarf was smoking a cigarette and I spotted the flashing lights of a sex shop. Istanbul, the Amsterdam of the Arab world, where you can stock up on porn and lube. I wanted to stop and shop in the worst cultural voyeur kinda way. What Turkish delights did they boast? Burka porn perhaps? Or was it more hard core?

It was especially intriguing because Morocco doesn't have sex shops, or that's what everyone told me, a foreign woman, anyhow. But, I'm positive they do. Because porn is second to food as the great unifier of world cultures. Maybe even the first. There's gotta be a guy in the far back dark alleys of the medina who's got a bootleg copy of Fatima Does Fez. Unfortunately, I started my quest to uncover Moroccan porn too late in the game to know definitively. And unfortunately, traveling with the elements means I can't always do all the world-changing undercover investigative porn reporting I crave.

When we finally made it to the apartment, the place consisted of five unheated rooms on five different floors connected by a slippery wooden stairway. I know because running down them with my socks on almost paralyzed me after flying through the air and landing flat on my back. The owner's personal effects were all over and effectively made it impossible not to feel like an intruder. It was awkward, like staying at your distant great aunt's house that you'd never met, but better than sleeping on the floor in an airport or in a tent with a lion outside.

Two days later, we headed back to the airport for an hour's flight to Cappadocia, a wonderland of veritable moon landscaping in central Turkey. Off to explore the centuries-old haven for Christians and ancient relics of cave dwellers. To get around, we needed a car. With a family of six, we can never take the economy car, requiring us to upgrade to a bigger car. How do Mormons travel anywhere? All they had was a tricked-out Mercedes van so cool Kanye West would have driven it. Or his chauffeur. But, we did, like we were chauffeuring the elements through the far reaches of the universe. Marking the second time the elements got the five-star treatment.

We stayed in a cave, The Legend Cave Hotel, and spent two days hiking the canyons and trudging through the ancient cave dwellings. We probably shouldn't have been traipsing all over antediluvian houses but we were Americans. If it wasn't roped off with several signs, an alarm system, a security guard and threats of federal prison time, that meant it was OK to trample and parade on through. It was only ancient history. History was yesterday's news and the future stopped at tomorrow.

On the second day, we headed further off the beaten path. To the tiny town of Mazi, we searched for Ihsan, the guide for the underground city there. Within two minutes of pulling into the small town in our celebrity mobile, we found him and headed to a cavern still being unearthed by local townsmen. Ice from the last frost covered the entrance like a welcome mat. We moved from room to room lit only by our flashlights, which the elements fought over.

"Would you like tea?" Ihsan asked with his Turkish hospitality at the end of our private tour.

"We were headed into town for lunch," Craig said.

"Mazi has no restaurants. You like barbecue?"

Craig and I looked at each other. "Yeah."

Ihsan escorted us out into the cold, windy, barren parking lot and started a fire out of a cardboard box. He singed his tools with the flame before he scurried to the market next door to buy vegetables, chicken and bread. The whole town gathered around to watch him cook for us, peering through the construction barricade. Unless they were just waiting to watch us eat. It was the Turkish Benny Hanna as he prepared lunch. Grabbing chairs from a desk in a nearby office, topping it off with a kilim rug, he urged us to eat.

It was without a doubt the best meal I'd ever eaten cooked in a cardboard box eaten in a parking lot in Turkey before and since. That was precisely the kind of travel we loved—dirty, rugged and real. That was what our travels were about…the quest to strip things down to core necessities and leave the rest behind. Extras only weighed us down physically and emotionally. We were synchronously stripping the barriers and distractions we'd let into our relationship too. Getting back to basics and the reason we got together in the first place. Because in the end, we both love the same things. Vintage and nostalgia. And our relationship was both, but now it was recycled and repurposed. With a future.

We paid Ihsan for the tour, the meal and a day full of memories. Then we packed ourselves in the van and headed back to the airport. Reluctantly starting the sojourn back to Istanbul. Urban life with its fast pace and crowds was draining.

~

If all this travel sounded adventurous and maybe even a little exotic, it was. But if I've given you the impression that traveling with kids was anything less than a whole bunch of whining strung together in some very cool and very public places then I haven't done justice to what that travel was truly like. It was completely exhausting. Our smiling vacation photos are big fat liars. They are the products of coercion and bribes.

Just as my eyes were opened to all manipulative people I'd gravitated to my whole life, came the realization that I couldn't rid myself of all of them. Namely, the elements. Who prayed on my over active sense of guilt. They had also mastered manipulation. There was no way for this recovering codependent to escape it. Mom guilt.

One of the first places we went in Turkey was Miniaturk. It was like Legoland with the great buildings of Turkey in miniature. Except it wasn't made of Legos and there weren't any rides and it was in Turkey. Other than that, it was exactly the same. Every little building had a podium where we swiped our tickets so automated robotic voices would tell us about the building. We didn't even have to read anything. Sounds super kid friendly, right? It was. It was just that the kids were completely obsessed by who got to the scanner to swipe their ticket first. And they would do anything, I repeat *anything*, to be first.

We took a boat ride on a dingy on the mighty Bosporus. Kids on a boat—how could that go wrong? Sky and Ember scored the front seats. River and Jade got the less desirable ones in the back. Now that was easy to remedy by switching the kids halfway through the ride, right? No. Because we were on the smallest, tippiest boat ever to set sail, so they would have been swimming in the mighty Bosporus. On second thought, maybe we should have tried that.

I was more than disappointed that we didn't encounter a single Turkish toilet in Turkey. I don't want to brag or anything but my whole family was damn proficient at squatting over a hole in the floor to do our business. It seemed very inauthentic to use a modern toilet in Turkey. To rectify the situation, I'll never refer to a squat potty as a Turkish toilet ever again.

We checked out the Basilica Cistern where water for the Great Palace had been stored in the 2nd Century. The kids asked a billion questions, as always. In theory, their curiosity should be encouraged. In reality, it was a pain in the ass. Because after we offered a lengthy explanation with one kid, the next kid (who had stood there the whole dang time) asked the exact same freakin' question. Followed by the next kid. And the next kid. And they did that every place we went. I didn't have enough patience in reserve; mine dried up two years ago. The final straw was when they kept asking how Medusa's big granite head got in the Basilica. And why it was upside down. That's when I exploded.

*"I don't know, OK! You're a reader! Here's the guidebook. Read it yourself!"*

Of course they were too lazy to open the book. I admit it felt good to shout and let them feel my wrath built during years of pent-up frustration.

We took the kids to a hands-on industrial museum complete with cars, trains and planes where they could touch everything. Besides each other, that was. The day we went, a large group of kids was there on a school field trip. No big deal, right? Except the elements were clustered together annoyed that the school kids were misbehaving, noisy and touching each other. What? And why wouldn't they split up? It was like they were stuck together by some unknown magnetic force. I think it was called abhorrence, unless it was animosity. Why was it always easier to see the annoying things other people did than to see your own?

All I wanted was a kilim or two. Turkish carpets were so cool, funky and fun. While I was lukewarm on Moroccan carpets, I could wallpaper my living room in kilims. When we stopped at a rug shop for a measly fifteen minutes, it suddenly became Wrestle-Mania time. The boys giggled and tore into each other the way boys do right before something gets broken or an ambulance was called. Not that I was concerned for their safety as much as I was for the gorgeous antique carpets. So we kicked them out of the store so they could settle it on the hard concrete sidewalk like men. Thankfully, no carpets were harmed. As a mother, I had to keep my priorities straight.

The day after a rainy afternoon kept us cooped up in the apartment without television or an iPod, which could only be described as hellacious, we went to an old fort. We let them run wherever they wanted without guardrails and with little supervision. We were exhausted. So exhausted that the kids won the battle to pet stray Turkish cats. In our defense, they were much less mangy than Moroccan strays. It was unlikely the kids would contract rabies and since they already acted crazy and foamed at the mouth, how would we know they had it? We should let them get all Lord of the Flies more often.

The day before we left we went to Topkapi Palace, the Louvre of Istanbul. Sky begged us to go because he'd heard they had the hair of the Prophet Muhammad on display. No one was more excited than me. I rushed through lunch and couldn't wait to get there. Butterflies in my stomach threatened to make me to throw up.

We waited in a long line to see the hair of Muhammad. I was suspicious that it was actually pubic hair and quite honestly, it could've been anyone's pubic hair. Who would know? That wasn't why I was excited. My girlfriends from Colorado, Linda and Mary and their families, would be there. They'd taken a cruise and ported in Istanbul during our vacation. For a whole ten minutes! We ran toward each other spotting each other in the overpriced museum cafe. It was a whole ten minutes my kids didn't fight, touch each other, complain, whine or ask questions. They were so surprised they barely uttered a word. Reminding me that travel was much more fun with friends. Don't leave home without them.

## TURKISH DELIGHTS

I completely neglected one huge part of our trip to Turkey—the food. I've been dying to talk about it but it was simply too massive. It had to have its own post. Everywhere we went the Turkish people were completely shocked we were American.

"You can't be American!" they said. "You are not fat!"

It was the most ass-backward, backhanded, non-delightful compliment ever. Especially hypocritical coming from Turkish people, who aren't exactly petite and boats the world's most lush unibrows. But who am I to judge?

Turkish delight is a jelly-like, bite-sized cube of fruits and nuts doused in powdered sugar. I thought it was kind of cool, albeit messy. But Craig and the elements didn't find any delight in it.

Bread dunked in oil. Leavened bread, not the flat bread I'd imaged for Turkey. Sometimes the oil contained chopped olives, sometimes spices. Sometimes both. Always delicious. The copious garlic always lingering on your breath for days afterward.

Roasted veggies. I know this sounds boring, unless your vegan, but I've never had more flavorful vegetables anywhere. Maybe it's because they grow them all in country under massive amounts of organic manure. I'm giving a special shout out to roasted jalapeños. Hollah!

Dairy. Unlike Moroccan cuisine, the Turks dabble in dairy. Breakfast is often accompanied by a rich and sumptuously salty feta. Thank god I'm not lactose intolerant because I would have spent the whole trip on a non-Turkish toilet.

Turkish kebab. Your choice of beef, chicken, lamb, or all three rolled into a flatbread with cabbage. Heaven. I would probably even oil wrestle a big 300 pound monobrowed Turkish dude to score one.

Baklava. The Greek influence is everywhere. A diabetes-inducing desert casserole of dough, honey and nuts. They even have a diabetic version because so many overweight Turks have Type 2 diabetes just like Americans.

Hummus. Every country in the region claims hummus as theirs. We wanted to send Sky to live in one of those other countries because he smelled so bad from eating so much of it.

The night before we left, we ate at the Istanbul Culinary Institute. Where I devoured a steak and onion tart. It looked like the bitter end of our trip until the server brought us free desserts. Then it was just the bittersweet end of our trip. Because Turkey, a place I'd never even considered before, had become one of my favorite places ever. And since I never got to go to the porn shop or the mud baths, I guess I'll just have to make a return trip someday.

On the way home, we had a nine-hour layover in Madrid, where we hit the town for the day. The people there were thinner, more fashionable and much more soft-spoken. I had some Spanish food washed down with sangria. My jeans were tight with a few extra pounds to fill out my size 0s. If I stopped plucking between my naturally shaped caterpillar eyebrows, I'd almost look a bit Turkish.

# Chapter 20

## Rainy Days and Mondays

Change brings with it trepidation, anticipation and depression. Everything was in flux. I was taking chances, revealing myself through my writing and abandoning fallacies of ever getting anywhere close to perfection in dance or anywhere else in my life. With Craig home more often, our marriage was slowly getting back to good. But, I knew even once we were on solid ground, cultivating a relationship worth keeping was arduous work that never ended.

It was the same with friendships. Early on, I'd started some defective, destructive ones, before I realized that's what they were. And that I'd subconsciously sought them out so I could self destruct in my own apocalypse. Finally realizing the only person I was deceiving was me. I'd become "that" girl, the one who had given up and let circumstances take the wheel. And I wasn't about to be that statistic at my 30 year high school reunion, the one I most likely wouldn't even go to. Not that anyone would notice. I was slowly accepting that potential I'd always denied I'd always had, back in the deep dark recesses somewhere.

Funny, I'd always been the cheerleader to everyone else in my life to believe in themselves. Especially the elements. I just never backed up what I said, by doing it myself. I was a false prophet. I'm still not a false prophet, cause I'm really not religious anyhow. And I can't proselytize because I have a fear of public speaking. Finally I wasn't a complete fraud for the elements. Although, I still couldn't help them with math. The burgeoning imperfectionist in me, could now say that without any shame. Just not on a stage in public.

Craig and I always tried to gently guide the elements and encourage them without controlling them. Ok, not always. There have been a million failings, fuck ups, shame and guilt inducing moments we've unintentionally inflicted on them. In my heart of hearts, I would really, really love to control them. But, let's be honest, I can't even get them to dress up nice with their hair brushed on that one pivotal day a year, school picture day. Honestly, I think lifelong photographic evidence of their rebellion will come back to bite them in their asses when they're 30 anyway. Style karma on kodak from decades gone by is a bitch to get over. Trust me, I had a mullet in high school and New Jersey mall hair with the claw in college. All their poor choices would come back to haunt them on their own. I didn't need to do anything to stop it. It's called natural consequences.

With the move almost upon us, I worried about the new delicate balance of our family and how a new geographic location could really screw with it. I had jurisdiction over my own issues and insecurities by then, and I was ready to continue to do battle with them. I knew that. But, I didn't have any authority over Craig's work schedule and all the other "what-ifs" when we got back to the States. I was more than capable of handling the kids on my own; I'd done that for years. Although I could endure it, I didn't want to anymore. I didn't need support; I craved it. And I didn't want to go through puberty alone. Again.

It was just another Saturday morning at baseball. It was also the meeting point to pick up Sky from a sleepover he'd had the night before at the house of a boy I disliked. He'd been invited on Thursday. International birthday parties in Morocco had the advanced notice of anywhere between three minutes to twenty-four hours. Americans knew that the correct social function incubation period was about three weeks. That gave you time to either come up with a thoughtful gift or plan a thoughtful excuse for not attending.

I was reluctant to let Sky go for so many reasons. Most of them started with Sky coming home from school saying something like, "Do you know what Nameless Douchebag kid did at school today?"

I didn't really want to know, except I kinda did in a morbid train wreck kind of way. On top of that, Douchebag's parents didn't speak much English. After twenty-four hours of anguishing over the right thing to do and contemplating every possible scenario that could go wrong, I decided to step back and trust my kid. They wouldn't be shooting heroin, right? I wanted to let him make his own choices. After I lectured him extensively, of course. To make sure they were informed, good choices. Hoping he'd make the right choice, not to go to Douchebag's party.

Baseball was the most boring sport known to man next to curling. To fill stagnant time, I chatted with the other disinterested lil slugger moms. That was what social people and those people pretending to be social did. We'd covered the important world politics of the day, like how many times we'd been puked on by our kids. When the game finished and River sat next to me. Recounting how many times Sky had barfed on me bored the shit out of him, so he rummaged through my purse for the gum hidden in the secret zipper pocket that was no secret to the elements. Then he waved a white baton like he was the grand poobah in a marching band and loudly interrupted us moms in the middle of our world peace solutions with a tampon. The secret zipper compartment also held my tampons. I guess the secret was out.

"What's this, mom?" he asked. Like maybe it was a fun dip candy stick he'd been missing out on or something.

I tried to subdue him and assure him I'll tell him later, when Douchebag's dad showed up with Sky. He was wired but fortunately lacked telltale heroin tracks on his arms. I checked. Praise the Lord, he was alive!

"Hey, how was it?" I asked.

"We were at the laser tag place til around midnight. Then we went back to Douchebag's house and didn't sleep all night!"

Oh sweet lord, today is gonna suck ass!

"Not at all?" It's for this very reason that I refer to sleepovers as sleepunders.

"I feel great. I'm not tired at all, Mom!"

Oh my god, maybe they snorted cocaine! That would explain the lack of marks and excessive energy on no sleep. "Well, did you eat breakfast?"

"Oh, yeah. Douchebag's dad gave us a bag of candy."

"OK so you didn't sleep and you ate candy this morning? You didn't sniff any pixie sticks, did you?"

"Oh, Brahim got all weird and called his driver to take him home in the middle of the night. Douchebag's dad didn't know until the morning."

"Alrighty, then. Well, did you have a good time?"

"No, not really."

Are you fucking kidding me? He shot kids with paint balls, stayed up all night and ate candy for breakfast while I stayed home with 3 envious kids and didn't sleep all night with worry and ate granola with disgusting Moroccan UHT milk? And HE didn't have fun? He'd begged to go. I'd driven him across town in crazy Friday afternoon mosque day traffic so he could not have a good time. I anguished over this and now he was destined to crash from his sleep deprived sugar high, thanks, and happy birthday, Douchebag!

After baseball, we rushed home for lunch. The mystery of the fun-dip tampon weighed heavily on River. He was relentless in the pursuit of the truth. He had resembled the Statue of Liberty when he'd held it up at the baseball field for all to see. So I gathered Sky, River and Jade to give them the lowdown while making tuna sandwiches. The irony of that didn't elude me. I gave them the nitty-gritty—tampons were not fun dip, they were inedible vaginal batons. And there was nothing fun about that. Or the fact that Craig was always off in Liberia or somewhere else whenever this puberty crap came up. Which is why I'm leaving teaching the elements how to drive up to him.

Sky was starting to detox right before I headed to my appointment at the spa. I'd left the elements alone in a foreign country, where I don't know what the hell the number for 911 was, to do it. It was Faith's fortieth birthday and the ASSs met to treat her to some pampering before the party thrown in her honor that night. Right before my Thai massage, Sky called. He'd hit rock bottom and it was ugly. Since I wasn't there I was spared witnessing it. I did what any exhausted mother would do. I said, "Sorry, gotta go honey! It's time for my massage. I'm turning my phone off now."

Thank god! I was free from frivolous calls from the elements about things like whether aluminum foil could go in the microwave.

I didn't usually treat myself to massages, so I'm unfamiliar with the protocol. Though we didn't share a common language, a tiny Asian woman instructed me to remove my clothes, gesturing for me to remove my underwear. Then I lay rigidly on a mattress on the floor wondering if the elements knew not to put aluminum foil in the microwave. Waiting to relax. With my eyes closed, I could clearly envision River pushing Ember off the trampoline. And even if they did figure out how to dial 911, the ambulances are nothing more than a taxi you can lay down in en route to the hospital. They're not even supplied with bandaids.

That's when the Asian woman started massaging my boobs. I couldn't stop myself from laughing until I snorted. She looked at me in horror. I tried to charade that my boobs were ticklish but I think I might have pantomimed "enraged gorilla beating his chest" instead. Ticklish is a tricky charade concept. After a lady I didn't know had reached second base with me, Faith, Jenny and I got our nails done. Even though I hate painted nails, they look like Easter egg talons, it was more fun than what was waiting for me when I got home.

Sky learned that when he crashed, he still needed to get his ass out of bed to endure a whole second party. An American party planned a whole month in advance that no one ditched early after snorting pixie sticks. When it was over, we all went home to our own beds and had a good night's sleep. Because a glass of wine, or three, does that to an old person. Americans over the age of forty with kids partied safely. Although, I know those days when the elements sneak out in the middle of the night while the old people are sleeping are close. Maybe next week even. I just don't want to be the one to have to get out of bed to drag their asses home and ream them. I'm more of a morning asshole reamer, person. Plus, that's a job best left for Craig.

~

Deja vu. We'd come to yet another goodbye season when bubblicious expats moved on to their next assignment in distant lands. I'm not gonna lie; there were acquaintances I was positively blissful to send off to Timbuktu and never see or hear from again. I won't miss wondering what the protocol is when someone disappeared for a couple of months, then resurfaced with two black eyes claiming it was allergies. When everyone knew she got her eyes done because they were so tweaked she wasn't Caucasian anymore, now she was Asian. She also suddenly and curiously lost 20 pounds. I suspect a magic wand was involved. Seriously, what are you supposed to say when people lie to your face? "Are you by chance allergic to the Japanese plum tree? 'Cause obviously you're not allergic to latex."

Or the guy who habitually sniff-snorted every thirty seconds. He seemed really intelligent and I'm sure he's a lovely person, but I was too grossed out to have a conversation with him. Then there's the couple that frequently fought fiercely and publicly who made social occasions even more excruciating than they already were. Actually, there were two of those. On the other side there was the bizarro family who's prized son could do no wrong gave Sky a hole in his eardrum. Then there was the chick who was so off, I was positive she had an undiagnosed mental illness. Rumor had it, she left her two small children alone in her car while she grocery shopped, and all alone unsupervised at home when she went out at night. Sadly, I won't be surprised if I see her name in headlines one day. Oddly enough, not everyone thought she was a cuckoo for coco puffs nut job. Or maybe they thought, I was the cuckoo for cocoa puffs one with an undiagnosed mental illness. But, I have been both diagnosed and labeled, thank you very much.

I was in good company. Jenny was OCD. Which meant having movers come to her house to touch her stuff, especially foreign movers, was a living nightmare. She wanted to do it all herself and blithely obsess over getting all her Cosby Show DVDs packed in the same box in sequence. And organized by the Cosby sweaters and yarn density worn in each episode. Unless she classified them by cotton and wool. Or color. I wasn't sure. I didn't want any part of that craziness. I am the antichrist of OCD and knew not to go anywhere near her or her house during the two days of packing.

I loved her and she loved me, but we were complete opposites. I left her organizational space alone, she tried desperately to ignore my cluttered and disorderly pantry and the rest of my unkempt house. But, when she was over at my house, she secretly salivated over reorganizing my unsystematic file cabinet. Healthy friendships were measured by knowing when to feed your friends' addictions and when to starve them. Everyone is fucking crazy in some way. It's picking the ones that compliment your crazy and hoping it tips the scales to be more benevolent than malevolent.

I kissed my ASS goodbye. It wasn't a long drawn out affair because we were all moving back to the States. Different states but even so, we'd still be neighbors of sorts. Just a drive down the road and a phone call away. I could text Jenny and Faith while buying large quantities of baby spinach at Costco. After an extensive two-year audition and weeding-out process, I was sure I'd found meaningful and enduring friendships. Ones that could withstand sporadic or even erratic neglect that was inevitable when friendships span long distances. If I called Jenny after not talking to her for two years, we'd talk just like old times while she organized her pantry and turned all the labels face out. The same with Faith. Although she would talk to me from the closet where she'd be trying to escape her boomslanging boys. Because Faith was so intolerant of farting she didn't do it herself. Which is seriously crazy because how can anyone refuse to fart without internally combusting?

I had bigger issues to contend with. Just when I thought things couldn't get worse, they did. It was bathing suit season.

## BATHING SUIT SEASON

In Morocco, women have lots of swimwear options. Although not quite as many as European women. Thongs and going topless were out. Almost anything else goes. Bikini, tankini, burkini. Whatever. Wait. You don't know what a burkini is?

A burkini is the aquatic friendly (I'm using *friendly* loosely) burka. Not that some women don't go swimming with their everyday *djellabas* and headscarves, 'cause they do. But if you've ever gotten pushed into a pool with your clothes on, you know they make drowning much more likely. So if you swim and want to be fully, completely covered without asphyxiating, a burkini is the way to go.

Claire saw them at Marjane and thought of me. Sara added that there were dressing rooms, so I could even try one on. It only sounds normal for a store that sells clothes to have dressing rooms, especially if you live in the States, but this isn't America. In Morocco, the necessity of knowing precisely where the olive bar is trumps the practicality of buying clothes that fit properly every time.

I went immediately to beat the impending rush. There it hung, essentially a wetsuit with a hood and a sassy peplum skirt that would create just enough drag to build a woman's biceps so she could milk a goat with utmost efficiency. By the way, did you know that veiled women can compete in beauty pageants in Morocco? How's that for an oxymoron?

Anyway, I found my size but I couldn't bring myself to try it on. Because the only thing blocking me from view was a flimsy plywood door between the bread and the luggage and a sketchy male security guard who stood directly in front of it.

Since in my extensive burkini comparison shopping, not, it appeared to be a reasonable price, I bought it. I'll get my money's worth because it solves a lot of problems. I don't need to shave or wear sunscreen. I don't have to shed those extra pounds I gained in Turkey. And every woman's worst fear? I don't have fret about forgetting to tuck in that damn dangling tampon string.

But. 'Cause you know there's a but. The one glaring problem? This modest swim attire doesn't have a modesty lining. Perhaps Moroccan men don't find the nipplage of a woman who has just exited cold water erotic. But I'm guessing they do. I bet it's far more of a turn-on than an uncovered shoulder or an exposed leg. So, modest? I don't think so.

If I do decide to swap my bikini for a burkini, do you know how ridiculous the tan line around my face from the hood is going to look?

# Chapter 21

## *H'mok* (Crazy)

A couple weeks before we moved, I was overcome with a crazy rage and infanticidal ideations. The culmination of our time in Morocco multiplied by being the mother of a teenager. Unless it was squared; I'm not good at math.

We'd just finished eating a spectacular gourmetish dinner I'd slaved over, which was ruined by the elements whining and subsequently rescued by wining. A delightful imported South African Pinotage, if you must know. After I reminded the elements several times to clear their plates, which required them to walk them clear across the house and into the kitchen, they mysteriously disappeared. When they returned to the dining room, Craig and I were still nursing our wine and winding down with a bitch session of how ungrateful the elements were. That's when they lined up *Sound of Music* style from youngest to oldest, to perform for us. Only their clothes weren't made out of curtains.

I don't remember what fire, earth and water did to entertain us. I'm sure it was heartwarming and something a mother should treasure forever. But, all I that remains of my foggy memory of that night was Sky's hand written monologue in his indecipherable chicken scratch. While the child loved to hear himself drone on, he hated to write. So, we listened with great anticipation. What could be important and exigent enough for him to write it down? Voluntarily.

"Our time in Morocco has flown by," he read. "I can't believe it's over. This was such an incredible experience...."

He went on for several more minutes with the most bullshit ever spewed out in one speech in history. I'm including presidential debates here.

My blood was boiling and I shook with rage, thankful that the long table protected him from me. Because all I wanted to do was use my steak knife to pole vault over it to him and strangle him slowly until every ounce of life was squeezed out of that child. In my head, it was a whirl of flailing arms, gagging, salvia and a little blood. Not too much because Mohammed had the following day off, which meant I'd have to clean it all up. And I still had the dinner dishes to do.

Don't get me wrong. I wanted him to be grateful and appreciative. But, I wanted him to be grateful and appreciative the entire two and a half years of it, not the last two weeks before we went home. It was way too little, way too late. Either that or it was way too soon. He should have waited until I was senile when I would have forgotten how hellacious he'd made daily living for all of us through his interminable complaining, grumbling, protesting, bellyaching, wailing and malcontent-ed-ness. God, I hope I'm senile before he learns to drive. If I don't kill him before he does. *Inshallah* (god willing).

~

Everything was running *h'mok*. Sky was suddenly cheerful and beholden but only because the end was near and we were moving back home. At least we wouldn't have to listen to him criticize and protest all things Moroccan anymore. Or witness his maniacal obsession over getting every grain of sand off his feet before we left the beach. Colorado didn't have beaches, thank god. But he was a teenager, so he'd find new things to deplore in America. We knew that. We were just looking forward to mixing up his monotonous bemoaning repertoire laced with dissent to include fresh new material.

River had grown his hair all the way to his shoulders and was adamant that he didn't want it cut. He'd been teased by classmates, constantly mistaken for a girl in public and it drudged through the food on his plate and dried onto it in little balls so it looked like he had lice. That might have been why he lost things so easily…because he couldn't see past the blond curtain. It was atrocious, but we bit our tongues. Until suddenly, without prompting, he wanted it gone. Not just cut, but buzzed completely off. Isn't a drastic hair cut a big literary symbol for metamorphosis and change?

Not to be undone by Jade's impending separation anxiety from Mohammed. She'd become known in our house as the Mohammed Whisperer because she was the only one of us who could communicate with him through an elaborate new language they'd created consisting of broken Franglais, some Darija and charades. She was his constant companion in the garden where she nurtured the plants and the turtles while she taught him English.

Ember had simply always been crazy. Fiercely competitive, insanely bold and much too smart for her own damn good. We'd hoped Morocco would soften her edges, particularly so she'd stop setting things on fire. That's not what happened, of course. Instead, she'd only learned to cover her tracks better.

Right before we left, I got the compulsion to hoard again. This time it was everything Moroccan. Lamps, carpets, jewelry and daggers. I was trying to take Morocco with me one piece at a time. What I wasn't doing was stockpiling my feelings anymore. No one was safe from my wrath. Especially the drunk belligerent guy who tried to mess with me on the boardwalk in Essaouira. When he wouldn't stop hassling Faith and I, I stepped up into his face and offered to fuck him up. I was strong, expressive and didn't need to rescue anyone else to feel worthy. And I certainly didn't require rescuing myself.

Although, backup was always appreciated. Since Craig spent more time at home while we were in Morocco, he was there to support the whole family. Physically and emotionally. Allowing us all to grow then reeling us back in when we needed it. Offering consistency and reliability. He did the important things that shouldn't get screwed up like arranging our stuff to be shipped home.

When the movers arrived, I hadn't done anything to prepare. For all our previous moves, I'd painstakingly organized and separated things. In the end, it never mattered and things got screwed up anyway. During this move things were bound to go awry, so I just accepted that they would.

The crew had all the standard moving accessories. Boxes, wrapping paper for delicate items, and tape that adhered to the lowest standards of stickiness. The worldly possessions acquired on our travels were slowly swaddled. Except for the picture of the King, which they oddly didn't wrap at all. Nothing was rushed in Morocco, which led me to believe they got paid by the hour. After running out of boxes and returning two weeks later with more, they loaded our possessions onto a flatbed truck. Completely unsecured and uncrated. Vulnerable and exposed to the elements. Not quite ready for the journey but getting shipped off anyway. Quite the way Craig and I were when we arrived.

~

Sara wasn't moving. She was staying in Morocco indefinitely. I didn't know when I'd see her again, so I was determined to soak up every final moment to last me until the next time we were in the same place at the same time. Saying goodbye to her was by far the hardest part of going. I'd spent years pushing people away so I wouldn't have to lose them later. Not anymore. So it stung like a bitch slap to the face to leave her .

Just like those pieces of Morocco, I'd carry pieces of Sara around with me. She'd be in my head encouraging me to push myself and use proper form when I did. Until I wanted to bitch slap her for consistently being so god damn relentlessly optimistic, supportive and encouraging. But, more importantly, she would always be in my heart, dancing through life with me and reminding me that dancing was anything but a frivolous waste of time.

Her birthday was dangerously close to if not on Mother's Day each year. So we kicked off the festivities on Friday afternoon with a lunch of twin Cobb salads al fresco before heading to hammam. While all the locals were trying to escape the hundred-degree heat, we were the only ones crazy enough to appease it in the sauna. Before we drove out to the beach for dinner.

We were feeling especially antagonistic so we snubbed the conventional Moroccan dress code. Opting instead for all-American sundresses that revealed cleavage and skimmed the bruised knees I'd earned at Sara's workouts. We didn't normally dress that way because it brought undo attention. As foreign women, we were already considered free-minded and liberal, which we were. But some Moroccan men wanted to get free-minded and liberal all night long with a foreign woman. While Moroccan women were expected to preserve their purity for marriage, the assumption was that American women were more akin to Jenna Jameson. I'd been cat called, followed, leered at and propositioned by enough Moroccan men to know.

But, we weren't hassled that night because we were on a double date with our husbands. And it helped that American men were on average taller and more intimidating than Moroccan men. But that's just generalizing and stereotyping.

~

For a few weeks, we'd lived out of suitcases in our big, empty mansion like rock stars. Just in time for the Mawazine Festival, an annual music festival that included African music, Latin music, and everything in between. The best part was that it was free. Rather, it was free to attend but was sung to a $12 million price tag. Which seemed like a misguided priority when roughly half the population was illiterate, less than half for women. But what do I know? Maybe paying Mariah Carey handsomely to sing will change that. Yeah, right. My ass.

The previous year, Craig and I had seen Yusaf Islam. You know, the artist former known as Cat Stevens. Moroccans loved him. I thought it was because he'd converted to Islam until everyone sang the words to Peace Train. But, when he performed his new material, you could hear crickets chirp. This year we'd see an American perform. It would be one of the last times I'd see Sara.

## UNFOCUSED

It started that morning. I was completely unfocused. I knew he was in town already and we would see him that night. Earlier in the day, Sara and I had worked out in the park. Surely that would take our minds off the anticipation. It hadn't. Because next to the walking path was the most upscale hotel in Rabat. We were sure that's where he was staying, so we decided to walk over and stalk him. Lenny Kravitz.

The plan was to dress rocker cool for the concert. Which is a totally uncool thing to do. Sara was delayed at a dance workshop and arrived at our house with her husband Christopher looking a bit disheveled. After years of dancing in musicals, she's unfazed by quick changes and chaos. Which must be how she managed to put on her makeup in Rabat traffic without impaling her eye with a mascara wand. We strolled in casually late and claimed our spots. Right behind the barrier of people who paid real Dirhams to get a whole twenty yards closer.

Late himself, Lenny finally strutted on stage. I could kinda see him from the little window created in the spaces between people's necks if I stood on my tiptoes. When that became too much of a literal pain in my neck, I watched the big screen. And took pictures, all of which were frustratingly out of focus. Rock stars don't stay still very long.

Then, two-thirds of the way through the concert, people started to leave. They probably don't know who he is because he doesn't have a son named Moroccan. Sara and I seized the opportunity to move closer. Leaving a gap between us and our husbands that was instantaneously absorbed by two Moroccan men who stood directly behind us. So closely behind I could feel a heartbeat on my back. So I arched my back and used my shoulders to force his chest off of me. That must have been too subtle because he placed both hands firmly on my thighs. I turned around and spewed, "Get your fucking hands off of me!"

He pretended he didn't know what the fuck I meant. It's common knowledge that women get assaulted in large crowds here. There were even rumors of rape at the Pitbull show a few days before. The Moroccan man-boys didn't know we had backup until Craig and Christopher pulled them off of us.

The last song Lenny played was a twenty-minute rendition of *Let Love Rule*. Then he left the stage and walked through the crowd. It became a mob scene as everyone pushed to get a glimpse of him. He looked like he was headed right for us when the guys pressed and thrust their bodies and junk on us again. Suddenly they knew enough English to say, "Pardon," but only because they knew we had reinforcements. Lenny headed back to the stage and the two men disappeared into the crowd.

Just two days later we disappeared, heading home.

# Chapter 22

## We're Comin' to America

Our flight landed in Chicago…unless it was Dallas. Airports all start to look the same after a while. We had to pick up our bags, go through immigration and customs then recheck our luggage for our flight to Colorado. Even though we were all both tired and wired from an extended layover in Paris and a long trans-Atlantic flight, the elements knew the drill. As we walked through the airport, an abrupt, obnoxious guy with a foreign accent started following us and asking us questions. Out of nowhere he had a microphone in his hand, a camera crew appeared and they filmed us. The elements were excited to finally be in a country where the language was English. So they'd talk to anyone. And they did.

"Where are you headed?" obnoxious guy asked.

The elements divulged the nitty gritty details of our travel itinerary to the annoying stranger while they wondered what TV channel their dramatic debut would be on. They'd returned to the States anxious for American TV, so the thought of starring on it was even more exhilarating than watching. I would have stopped them but I was too exhausted. Plus, it kept them entertained and distracted from fighting over who had to pull the heavy suitcase with the bad wheel. I didn't know what he wanted or why and I didn't care.

Until we discovered that he wanted to give our family a free trip somewhere right then and there. We would simply roll our battered and bruised luggage to a different gate, get on a plane and go on vacation somewhere else. If we hadn't already been on an extended vacation for the previous two and a half years, we totally would have gone. At that moment, the only place we wanted to go was home. Later, I would totally regret passing up an opportunity for travel and adventure. Sometimes, when I wake in the middle of the night, I still wonder where obnoxious guy would have sent us. Even though there were more exploits to come when we got home.

~

Just like that we were back in Colorado. I'd been dying to broadcast the scoop on embassy life for a long time. Now that I was safely back on American soil, it's time to divulge all its secrets. Including how subversive the culture was, how fake the people were and how destructive it was to the American dream. I'm speaking of course of the Embassy Suites hotel.

Before we'd left for Morocco, while all of our possessions were packed in boxes and we prepared to move to Africa, we'd stayed at the Embassy Suites for a week. Because our house was empty and it was the cheapest hotel option for a family of six at $99 a night. When we discovered that our house in Colorado wouldn't be ready to move into immediately, we knew exactly where to stay. How perfect it was to go full circle and stay at the same place where we'd started this whole experience. No matter that it was now $139 a night. It was still the best deal in town.

We arrived at the Colorado Springs airport after two days of travel. My friend Kirsten and her kids Quinn and Molly met us at the airport. Overcome by sentimentality, sleep deprivation and the helium balloons they'd brought, despite a massive helium shortage no one knew or seemed to care about, I sobbed. After renting a car, schlepping our bags to the hotel, checking on our house, running to the grocery store, swimming in the hotel pool and happy hour, we simply couldn't stay up any longer. It was 6:30 p.m. Which of course meant the following morning would begin much too early.

We were up before the annoyingly chirpy sing-songy birds and yet were still so tired we couldn't wait for breakfast to have our first euphoric cup of coffee. So we made it in our room. The same room filled with environmental propaganda on how green the hotel was. After tearing open the plastic wrap with two individual pods of coffee, two stir sticks and too many packets of sugar and creamer (Craig has a sweet tooth), the coffee dispensed itself into two disposable cups. They even had those very American coffee sleeves because god forbid some dumbass doesn't realize that coffee is hot and burns their hand then sues or something. I forwent the sleeve and singlehandedly saved the rain forest one sliver of a tree. I'm sure that sliver was repurposed from coffee sleeve to Ikea packaging anyway. Oh, well. I tried.

After we took our extra-long, extra hot showers to wash away the travel funk because unlimited water wasting came free with the room, we followed the herd to the free breakfast buffet. That was where we really got our money's worth. If you put Fruit Loops, donuts, chocolate milk and pancakes in front of my kids and tell them they can eat as much as they want from the hours of 6:30 a.m. to 10:30 a.m., they will gorge like starving children in Africa. Which they would tell you they'd been just the day before. Then they'll go back for a second breakfast right before breakfast ends like the deviceful, insatiable American kids they were.

We didn't discourage this, of course, because everything they consumed reduced the price of our stay. So we ignored the fact that this kind of gluttonous consumption increased obesity, which in turn increased the cost of medical care. It was the American way and we're in American now. After breakfast, we pledged to take the stairs to undo all the damage. But, they were inconveniently hidden somewhere, so we took the elevator instead.

Our first few days were spent registering the elements for school, buying a washer and dryer, establishing an internet connection, getting archaic cell phones with the smallest buttons available that require me to wear my reading glasses to text, and braving the crowds at Walmart. After that we really needed to relax and unwind. Of course, Embassy Suites had us covered. Happy Hour was from 5:30 p.m. to 7:30 p.m. and we could have as many preservative filled snacks originating from a can or a bag, half of which was air, as we wanted washed down with as much liquor as we could drink. For free. Luckily, red wine is good for heart health. Maybe it would counteract the morning's bacon. If research said one glass was good, more must be even better. Isn't that the American way?

We were tempted to let the elements have a sip so they would sleep better but we weren't in Europe. In America, we could have been arrested for that. We settled on Shirley Temples knowing it was stupid and counterintuitive to sugar load sleep-deprived kids right before they went to bed in a room we unfortunately cohabited with them.

Between the breakfast and the happy hours, not to mention the marathon high-velocity scorching showers and all the water the elements splashed out of the pool, they weren't making any money from us. They were actually paying us to stay with them. Which was why we extended our reservation and stayed one more night until our kitchen items arrived. Except there was no room for us. They were completely booked. Which explained how they stayed in business—businessmen. One to a room. Yes, of course, it was the law of averages.

So what's my point? You can get a great deal at the Embassy Suites but every happy hour ends. When it does, it will cost you. At the least, a trip to the cardiologist.

## BURKA IN AMERICA

When I did the first burka post six months ago, I knew there would be another one. One that would be far more scary because I would be anything but invisible. And for six months, whenever I thought about it, I'd get anxious and contemplate all the things that could possibly go wrong. Then I thought maybe I shouldn't do it at all. But, I always thought that wearing a burka in America would be the more interesting social experiment. So I knew I had to.

I live in middle America...Colorado Springs to be exact. It's a little bit country, a little bit rock and roll, and a whole lotta evangelical Christian headquarters. This is no melting pot. (Although we do boast the downtown fondue chain.) This is homogeneous-ville. Not by design but by some weird magnetic force that draws pale-as-whole-milk churchy people here. Of course I'm overgeneralizing. Well, kinda. Have you been here? My point is, I have never, ever seen anyone in a burka within the city limits or anywhere else in the state. It's just something that doesn't happen here in the West.

I knew the perfect place to conduct such an experiment, the most American place on earth besides Disney World—Walmart. In the middle of the day, in the middle of the week. I didn't know exactly what to expect. I imagined some stares, pointing, whispering, and a bit of instantaneous contempt. Again I'm overgeneralizing but in situations like this, all it takes is one person to make things go horribly wrong. That's why Craig came with me. Not "with me" with me but watching from afar to make sure I was safe. That and someone needed to take pictures for the blog. But, mostly for the safety thing though.

My legs, wobbly with nerves, carried me through the parking lot past two men standing outside the entry doors. I tried to make eye contact but they averted their gaze. Until I passed them and saw the reflection of their turned heads aimed directly at me in the glass. The greeter sat in her motorized cart stunned into silence so I didn't receive the gratis welcome owed every customer. Except me.

I started in produce, where I noticed the greeter rolling along in her motorized cart behind me. And she was not rolling back prices; she was eager to get a closer look. Maybe she wanted to run me over because she drove dangerously close and narrowly missed crashing into my cart. Or maybe that's just how she rolls. She followed me down two more aisles before either losing interest or suddenly remembering her vital greeting duties.

I settled into shopping for groceries. Careful to not buy the bacon that could blow my cover. With each aisle I grew more relaxed because no one was looking, staring or pointing. Yet I wasn't invisible either. If a cart was in my way, other shoppers politely moved it and apologized for the inconvenience, the way Americans do. I was neither invisible nor a spectacle. Which is not at all what I'd expected.

I made it all the way to the back of the store in the dairy section without so much as a second glance. I was just another one of the freaks of Walmart. Although, my rating on the freak scale was rated pathetically low compared to the photos of the people of Walmart online. So no one cared or glared. Maybe Walmart wasn't the right venue after all. This was going nowhere fast. I had to do something. So I started talking to people.

"Have you had that yogurt before?" I asked while fondling a Greek. Yogurt that is. "Is it good?"

My fellow dairy lover looked right into my eyes and explained with a smile how delicious that flavored Greek yogurt was without a blink. Later, that key lime flavored one would prove her right.

Now, this is the point where Craig got bored, started shopping and lost track of time. Walmart can do that to you in a very Gruen transfer way. Which is funny because out of the two of us, Craig was far more fearful for my safety. It had just become a routine Walmart run with me wearing a burka.

I walked the rest of the way through the store asking employees where to find chalkboard chalk (which I never did find), stovetop cleaner, those frozen ice cube sheets for coolers, anything I could think of to engage people. I also continued to chat up customers. Then I slowly perused the toy section where I was sure a small inquisitive child would be enticed to say, "Is that Darth Vader's wife, mommy?"

But no. Apparently even kids have seen those people of Walmart YouTube videos and know I didn't compare to people shopping sans pants with a grossly outdated Billy Ray Cyrus mullet and sheepskin vest. After a couple hours of extremely slow and methodical shopping in a burka, I was done. I simply couldn't think of anything else to do or shop for and it had become boring. I texted Craig to abort the mission and headed for the checkout. Hoping something would happen so I'd have something to write about. Maybe I would use my credit card and the cashier would check my ID and ask to see my face for proof of me-ness. Of course, she didn't. She was friendly as could be. Until I left the store and she ran into the parking lot behind me shouting to get my attention. Turns out, I'd left my eggs in the revolving bagging wheel.

Craig met me at the car. We were both stunned that there had essentially been no reaction. Maybe if I'd done it on a weekend or at a different store. Maybe I should've gone to Hooters to attempt to eat some wings. Maybe if I'd worn the thicker face veil that hid my facial expressions. Or maybe if fewer people buried their heads in their cell phones and looked up once in a while. Or maybe, just maybe, Americans were more tolerant or at least more politically correct than I gave them credit for.

# *Chapter 23*

## Going to Extremes

Colorado was normally dry this time of year. This summer, it was both extremely dry and unusually hot. We'd heard about all the wildfires out west before we'd returned from Morocco. We just hadn't thought it would affect our neighborhood. No one ever does. Until Saturday when a fire started extremely close to us.

Instead of packing things up and evacuating, we breathed the fresh paint fumes that filled our house after two days of having colored our world. We tried plum in the living room, which turned out to be more grape jam. Before resorting to cranberry, which was still too redolent. Spicy cayenne had just the amount of heat we'd been looking for without becoming an inferno, which we were hoping wouldn't become the fate of our house.

Saturday was also Jade's eleventh birthday. She'd invited four girlfriends to sleepover at our house still filled with boxes. But, my one kid who never asked for anything didn't get that party because three of those girls evacuated. Instead of being disappointed, Jade was concerned that the city had left piles of dead branches behind our property after cutting them down to curb the mistletoe infestation, combined with the moving boxes strewn about, making our house a tinderbox.

We watched the fire for two days. Waited for a mandatory evacuation with little else to do besides unpacking and home improvement projects. Which is ironic, considering that we were in imminent danger of not having a house to improve. The kids were hot, bored and frustrated because many of their friends had already skipped town. It was a hundred degrees, we didn't have air conditioning and the pool we frequent was closed due to the fire threat and subsequent smoke fumigating the west side of town. Frankly, I was more worried that the elements would kill each other than of the wildfire.

Days passed like that. Until Tuesday. By then, we were used to the campfire smell of burning ponderosa pines. The familiar smell had the elements begging for marshmallows but I didn't cave. Instead, I got my biannual haircut with my derby pal Snow White Trash, before the kids and I and some friends headed to the pool that had just reopened. A typical summer day.

The pool is nestled in a valley neighboring Garden of the Gods and the Rocky Mountains, offering stunning views. On that day, it also provided a front-row view of the action. Smoke plumes billowed over the ridge, a testament to nature's duality. Serenity and fury, pleasure and pain; the eternal courtesans.

C-130s and helicopters flew directly overhead attempting to combat the inferno. While the kids swam, we moms watched the beautifully choreographed air assault, snapping photos of the airshow. Urging the girls to save some snacks for the boys who were waging their own water assault.

Suddenly, in a furious gust of Colorado wind, the flames crested the ridge. Kirsten, Birgit and I stood motionless watching it rage down the hill. Until our friend Linda called and urged us to leave. Now. Scrambling to collect all our kids, it struck me that maybe I should have packed something ahead of time. Important documents.

The elements' adoption paperwork, at least. But I hadn't done anything, the road out was blocked, Jade was crying uncontrollably and the gas tank read empty. I'd had to find a new way home to collect our things. A longer, unfamiliar one that diverted us away from the fire then directly back toward it. Craig made it home before us and was already packing vital documents and the two crap computers that had already been fried by the sporadic surges of electrical currents in Africa. Every element was instructed to pack some of their clothes into a bag as quickly as possible. Jade was inconsolable. I wanted to wrap my arms around her and tell her it would all be ok. Which was a lie I didn't have time for.

Craig insisted we drive two cars and that I take Jade, Sky and Ember. He'd stay and finish packing up with River. I thought it was stupid to split the family up, but I did it anyway. Leaving with no idea where I was going except away from the fire. The sky was dark with ash and smoke, making it appear it was closer to midnight than late afternoon and required I turn on the headlights. The ash drifted down in giant fluffy snowflakes. I called Craig's cell to make a plan but couldn't get through, the network was flooded.

Cars were at a standstill, lined up single file and equidistant from each other on the main street out of the neighborhood, which was surprisingly neighborly considering the urgency to escape the impending threat. No one cut me off or honked and no one appeared to be in any rush. I was the only offender. The young woman in the car next to me rolled down her window to ask in the most genial way that I not crowd her. I hadn't even realized I was doing it. We'd only been home for two weeks, I hadn't yet reacclimatized myself. I was just driving Moroccan-style.

I tried to feign a calm demeanor for the elements, but the fact was we were running on fumes and kids can smell fear, just like dogs. Finally, I reached the pump. Only, the gas lines had been shut off throughout the whole community. We'd have to forge on, not knowing if we'd make it to the next station.

I reached Craig after dialing furiously and repeatedly like a teenage girl trying to win free concert tickets to see her favorite boy band from a radio station. We had a plan, he'd meet me half way. At the next gas station, I fueled up with the rest of the slackers who hadn't made evacuation preparations and continued east to our rendezvous point. We're grateful to be together and alive. For about an hour before it returned to the standard summer night of sibling squabbles driving to the only available hotel. In Pueblo.

Where we once again crammed our family of six of us into one tiny hotel room, the only available one for miles, strewn with our baggage we'd travelled the world with. That's where Sky showed us the contents of his hastily packed luggage. It included some clothes, no underwear, and the family photos that sat next to the fireplace he hastily snatched on the way out the door. Craig and I. Our parents' wedding photos. Pictures of his siblings; the elements of our world.

While Craig and I made so many mistakes in our marriage, we'd finally got it right. During our misadventures in Morocco, we'd learned to trust and rely on each other. Realizing what should have been obvious all along, we're better and stronger together than apart. Underneath all the sibling squabbles and the all years of distant togetherness, we'd never stopped being a family that loved and supported each other. Even at our worst.

~

It was probably best that we hadn't found a hotel in the Springs and brought our passports. While Pueblo was only a forty-five minute drive south, it was a world away. We had friends there, an old war buddy of Craig's named Laura. Although our problems started piecemeal long before Craig was deployed, the fifteen months he'd spent in

Iraq while I stayed in Germany with three small kids, made the wedge deeper. It forced my already fierce independence into overdrive. It all made sense…textbook, really.

In the years since Iraq, Laura married and had two kids of her own. The day we saw her was her oldest daughter's second birthday. They'd welcomed a new son just a few months earlier. A young family, as we'd once been. Her kids were a year younger than the elements were when Craig became a long-distance husband and dad. It'd taken almost ten years and almost losing it all, to bring us back to the family we once were. Except we were different, because no one can be exactly who they used to be, nor should anyone want to.

When a hotel room closer to Craig's work opened up a couple of days later, we moved back to the Springs. We also wanted to be nearer to our home, even if we weren't allowed back yet. There was something comforting in being near it. Closer to the action, even though we weren't able to help the fire fighters as they continued to battle the blaze that was even now, only partially contained. Deciding to live life normally and buy a new car, the only one we've ever owned, and lizard-sit for a friend, until the hotel kicked us out and we were homeless once again.

A friend of a friend invited us to stay at their house. I normally wouldn't accept an offer to stay with someone I barely knew, but we weren't normally not homeless and void of other options. So we stayed with strangers who after one night became our friends. How were we to know then that the next year during the Black Forest fire, when their home was threatened, we'd be able to repay the favor.

When the gas lines were secured and we were allowed back to our house the next day, it was untouched. It didn't even smell like smoke. The only issue, a massive one, was settling it had done while we'd been in Morocco. Our house was slowly sinking into the unstable Colorado soil, splitting floors, preventing windows and doors from closing. Insurance wouldn't give us a dime for the earth swallowing our house. Financially, we'd have been better off if it had burned to the ground. But, we didn't want to live anywhere else.

I don't know if I'd noticed it before we moved to Morocco or not. Either way, I'd taken it for granted. Then when some of our neighbors' homes were ravaged by the inferno, the flames couldn't burn it. Instead, they ignited and it spread like wildfire. Community. Everyone lives in a neighborhood but not every neighborhood has a sense of community.

When we'd bought the house seven years before, we hadn't realized the investment we'd made. Even more prodigious than our financial debt was the emotional investment in our neighborhood. That was where I'd stalked the parents of my kids' best friends until they finally gave in. As if they had a choice. Their kids are some of my kids' best friends. And while they are growing up so quickly, they still play a game of twilight hide and seek now and again. The elements can walk next door to Carol's house for some honorary grandma time. Bonus, she's much more crafty than me, cause I'm not crafty at all. My kids walk to school right down the road. We know each of their teachers and none of them yell.

My friend Hillary started a community garden where we can all plant and nurture seeds and each other, with the help of a little sun and a little rain. My friend Lynn, one of those kindergarten moms I diligently hunted, lost her house in the fire. Months later, she bought a new house in our old community. I asked if I could help her move in, it seemed the neighborly thing to do. Stupidly forgetting that everything she owned now fit in her car because everything else had gone up in flames. So we threw her a shower complete with two fire fighters, a new junk drawer and a killer sound track that included *Burning Down the House*, thankful that she was staying in our tight-knit community.

## THE UNTHINKABLE

I'm addicted to books. Which is an expensive addiction when you live overseas and don't have a local library. Now that we're back stateside, you can find me at the library scouring the new arrivals shelf stockpiling armfuls of books. I'm particularly enamored with nonfiction, especially psychology and sociology. A couple of weeks ago, I spotted a captivating title. *The Unthinkable: Who Survives When Disaster Strikes and Why.* Intrigued, I piled it on top of my already looming stack.

I didn't think about how timely it was to read a book about disaster after the Waldo Canyon Fire. Probably because it was too soon to make sense of it. So I put it in the rotating reading queue in my head. Which happened to be right after another book on writing. Before I got to it, the unthinkable happened. The Aurora shootings. Overnight, reading this book became a priority.

After the flames crested the ridge in the Waldo Canyon Fire and we evacuated, I'd been struck by the complete lack of panic. Some people didn't evacuate at all but instead climbed on their roofs in the pseudo-night sky while it rained ash to glimpse the inferno and take pictures. The traffic exiting our neighborhood, threatened by flames, was overtly orderly and polite. I remember thinking how completely bizarre that was. Surely that wasn't a typical reaction to an impending disaster. Turns out, I was wrong. It is.

It's one of the most powerful coping mechanisms humans have. It's coping's powerful first responder: Denial. Not that I would know anything about denial. Because I was lounging at the pool without any bags packed staring at the crest of the ridge when it happened. Taking pictures. Before Linda called and ordered us to leave. That's when fear set in. I didn't know it at the time but statistically fire is by far the biggest threat to all of us and claims more lives each year than any other catastrophe. In a world full of other, more blockbuster-worthy threats, who'd think fire? Though there seems to be cataclysmic events the world over these days, your chances of being in one are extremely small.

As counterintuitive as this sounds, knowing what to do in the event of a cataclysmic event decreases your stress. We can't predict our behavior in a crisis because it's far more primal than we might realize and hides deep within the brain in the hippocampus. If you have one as big as a hippo, it will increase your chance of survival. As will not wearing high heels.

The book made a greater point. In a world where so many things beyond our control stress us out, why do we have blinders on to the really imminent mortal threats? The choices we make daily put us at more risk than anything else. Our lifestyles.

1. Heart disease
2. Cancer
3. Stroke

Statistically, these are the three things most likely to kill you and the ones you love. There are three things you can do to reduce your risk right now—eat a healthy diet, exercise and quit smoking. Slap on some sunscreen and you've got four. Don't let the unthinkable happen to you.

*Addendum: While writing this book, I came to view the fire as a metaphor for my troubled marriage, fleeing to Morocco (complete with denial, panic, getting back to basics) and ultimately the journey as a family back to safety.*

# Chapter 24

## T-Shirts, Trophies and Tiaras

Before we even left Morocco, I knew it had to be one or the other. Either my old love roller derby or my new love belly dance. I wish I didn't have to choose because I loved them both for different reasons. But, with conflicting practice schedules, not to mention four kids whose social agendas trumped mine and a marriage I wanted to keep, I knew I had to choose.

I thought I had this figured out and the clear winner was belly dance. I cyber stalked an instructor with the very unexotic American name, Barb, a couple months before we moved back. Watching her YouTube videos and trying to get a feel for her through my computer screen. Her friendly and welcoming, but not too auspicious facebook page convinced me she was the one. Someone I could see myself being friends with. Which sounds like my old codependent fast friends self. Now I'm looking for slow cooker, crockpot kind of friends, where the ingredients have time to simmer into just the right layers of complex flavors. So I figured her friendship was on my 10 year layaway a friend plan. Bonus, she taught in English. Even though I had no idea what the name of any particular move was in English.

Then something happened. Rather, a few things happened. I saw my roller derby wife, Mama Beast, for the first time since my return. She'd just hung up her skates and retired from roller derby like I did a couple of years before. The memories of my glory days, or non-glory days of picking myself up off the floor after another beating, flooded back.

"MurdeRita died." she told me.

"What! How? What happened?"

"She collapsed and died. No one knows why yet. The funeral's in a couple of days. Pepper Slay and some other derby girls are going."

Mama Beast, MurdeRita, Haila Bullets and I all started skating at the same time, members of our own exclusive Orange Wheel Club named for the rented skates we used until we were able to buy our own. Rita was married and in her thirties with a thriving career and three young kids. She was healthy and vibrant with her whole life ahead of her. Until the day she died, suddenly and unexpectedly. She was a tragically intimate reminder that life is fleeting. Whatever your "it" is, do it now.

That Saturday my Beastie and her fiancé, Craig, the elements and I sat in the stands and watched the roller derby bout. I wanted to bite down on my mouth guard while skating the track's curves, take the outside and slalom back to knock a bitch to her knees clean to the inside of the track. That was my fantasy. Only a fool took the outside and my mouth guard was big, obtrusive, and tasted like the Listerine I soaked it in and it made me drool uncontrollably. I wanted to wear my bruises like trophies again. Nostalgia is a powerful drug.

There was no time to waste, so I started belly dance class a couple days after we arrived while we were still staying at the hotel. Barb was teaching a sword dance. Yeeeeeeeeesss! I'd only seen it on YouTube. Even though belly dance originated near Morocco, dancing with a sword balanced on your head is an American invention. It was part of our national quest to make things more entertaining by making it more dangerous. And I totally wanted in.

~

We'd only been back about a month and a half, yet I was consumed with reminiscent thoughts of Moroccan summers gone by. Back in America, there were a million things to do and the elements wanted to do them all today. They complained about not having done them yesterday and planned to cram it all in tomorrow. Last summer they'd made weapons out of sticks and duct tape, bored out of their minds, but despite that, they were happy. This summer we lived in the land of t-shirts, trophies and tiaras. Where kids didn't play with sticks and happiness could be bought. Or could it? Where every kid's activity has a mandatory snack, a free t-shirt, a trophy or a free coupon for a kid's meal at Chick-fil-A. Worst case scenario, a tiara was at stake.

The elements transitioned back into American life seamlessly, in about a week. While I suffered an extended reverse culture shock and repeatedly sobbed at grocery stores because I was overwhelmed by the fast pace of life and endless choices that had to be made in the land of opportunity. I thought maybe the elements would have an epiphany, any day now, that they didn't need stuff to be happy. Maybe they could be content in an X-box and iPhone-free world. They weren't, and I was pissed. I wanted to start the whole gratitude lesson plan over again with a move to another undeveloped country. Preferably a warm one but not warm enough that we'd want air-conditioning. Laos maybe. Bhutan? Wait. Bangladesh!

Suddenly, every drink required ice. Despite somehow having survived just fine without it for two years. Albeit, their thirst had been quenched at room temperature.

When we bought our new minivan, we had to work out a schedule for who sat where to combat constant sibling seating squabbles. Gone were the days when we'd owned only a banged-up piece of crap car that looked luxurious in a sea of mopeds and donkeys. We should have bought a goat instead. How multipurpose would that be. It could be our transportation and the elements could milk it to make cheese.

The elements constantly asked to watch TV. We had a seemingly endless channels, while there was always something on, most of it was crap. I missed what a pain in the ass it was to download shows from the internet. It made *Dirty Jobs* way the hell more dirty, rewarding and infrequently watched.

Then there was shopping. The elements never wanted to shop in Morocco and neither had I. Now they wanted to come with me so they could beg me to buy things for them. Specifically electronics, anxious to discover the latest useless trends to connect with their friends who were sitting at home in front of a screen, eating cheetos and blowing things up. Video games, cell phones and social media made destroying their reputation and flushing their future down the toilet virtually instantaneous. At least keeping them inside glued to a screen kept them off the streets and out of harms way from the kidnappers and drug dealers. So there's that. I longed for days shopping in Marjane where there was nothing worth longing for and the biggest threat to the elements was getting run over by a donkey if they didn't look both ways before crossing. And who's the ass if that happens?

Our fridge was stocked top to bottom, crammed full of Costco-sized portions. "There's nooottttthhhhhiiiinggg to eat!", they whined. I wanted to stuff thirty cheese sticks down their collective throats. What was I thinking? All this food was going to go bad before we could eat it all. Wait. Nevermind, it's all filled with preservatives, and mold doesn't grow on cheese here, it'll last forever. Our fridge in Morocco had been sparse, barren even. Yet there was always something to eat, usually an olive or a date. Which meant you only ate when you were so hungry you considered gnawing off your own arm.

Don't even get me started on cell phones. They were the social status maker of their generation. Back in my generation, it was Nike sneakers. Which I never had growing up and I survived with only minor scaring. Cell phones fed into parental paranoia, without one someone would steal our kids. Or they wouldn't be able to get ahold of us to ask us the really big important questions like, "Mom, what's for dinner?" Seriously, who would steal a kid who's not cool enough to have their own cell phone, who's having creamed spinach for dinner?

Had they learned nothing in Morocco? Was I the only one who'd been transformed? That's it! We need to move to India. It was impoverished, dangerous but with balmy weather and amazing vegetarian food, insuring they'd eat their vegetables. And they spoke British English, which was a foreign language, and we didn't know anyone there so my kids wouldn't need a cell phone to talk to their nonexistent friends.

I don't know if we'll move overseas again. It was the best thing I'd ever done for my family, my marriage and myself. Morocco changed me. I'm stronger now. Allowing myself to be frivolous gave me focus. Writing transformed me into someone both visible and vulnerable. Imperfect and irreverent. I'm not consumed with inadequacy and depression, the old bedfellows who used to hold a *ménage a trios* with my perfectionism. Although my default setting is still set for invisibility and taunts me. I don't have to succumb to it anymore. I've changed my old ways, shedding some of my toxic paramours; I'm different now.

I don't know if anyone else notices it, nor does it matter. I see it and I feel it in everything I do. I'm willing to take risks and make mistakes. It took my forty some years to get here to self acceptance. I want things to be different for the elements. I don't want them to struggle and doubt themselves. I want them to set their own course and know their own power, no matter where in the world they are. Right now that's America and it's that pivotal time of year, election season.

## BE THE CHANGE

Last night was another evening of math homework with the elements. I may have mentioned before that I'm not good at math. "Not good" being an understatement. Because of that, I pass anything to do with numbers off to Craig, which of course includes science. But I'm the go-to person for English and social studies. So when Sky told me his homework was to watch the Democratic Convention, I was on it.

What you might not know is that I have a degree in political science. You wouldn't know that because generally I don't talk politics. I'm not interested in converting you to my political beliefs or my religion or lack of it for that matter. At the dinner table, it's a whole other matter. We talk about everything and that has always been the case.

While Sky and I watched and discussed the conventions, I thought about how our time in Morocco shaped the elements. How that was the one time in their lives they'd been the minority. And how they'd been bullied for having different beliefs. How I'd cried for them but beamed with pride as they'd held their ground and stood up for themselves. Hoping it would build their character, tolerance and understanding. Hoping for change.

Suddenly, change did come to North Africa. Revolution was everywhere. You could feel the excitement and the uncertainty in the air. With Tunisia in turmoil, Egypt under military rule, Osama Bin Laden dead then Gadhafi, what would become of Morocco? No organization was organized enough to overthrow the government. Then, quietly, constitutional reform was instituted by the King and a parliament was born.

Except, while there'd been so much hope for change, the changes had turned out to be underwhelming. Egypt traded Mubarak's corruption for an Islamist regime. Granted, one where a woman could deliver the news in a *hijab*. And while the King of Morocco reformed the constitution, he remains the country's supreme authority on Islam and the commander of the military. He also has the power to dissolve the parliament at any time. That's just the beginning of a long process that takes diligence and resolve. At times it's slow and stalls. Eventually with diligence, time and hard work it'll happen.

I would know. Not only was change spreading throughout North Africa but North Africa had spread change throughout my family.

*Addendum: After my ridiculously small pastry sharing married acquaintance from that fateful cafe back in Morocco read this post and the term "Islamist regime" she stopped reading my blog. While we can each "be the change", we're each going to have different opinions and ideas about what those exact changes are. If we even want to make them at all. Which is why change can be such a solitary venture than can cause us to lose friends and ridiculously distant fleeting acquaintances. Be the change anyhow. Knowing new friends, ridiculously distant acquaintances and adventures await.*

# Chapter 25

## Unhappily Ever After

Since we were managing a transcontinental move on our big day, we postponed celebrating our anniversary. We'd been back in the states for six months. This trip would be a much needed break from Craig's work and my book writing, belly dancing and my newest addiction, pole dancing. We'd worked at such a frantic pace to get settled, we needed to make time for us. We always did. That was our fatal flaw. We allowed the constant stress in our lives to drive us apart.

When we'd met nearly twenty-five years earlier in Holland, we were young students who didn't know what the hell we were doing starting what would be a four-year long-distance romance. Since this was the late 80's with no internet, cell phones or anything pixelated, we wrote letters every day to bridge the gap. Saving the expensive weekly phone call for Sunday, when the rates were cheaper because we were poor college students. The month after I graduated, we got married. With all the big Catholic 80's trappings, big teased out hair with poofy sleeves and lots of standing, sitting and kneeling for no apparent reason. Having never spent more than two weeks together at a time. We were young, naive and stupid. We didn't know that 60% of couples married between the ages of twenty and twenty-five divorce. Even if we did, it wouldn't have mattered. We were never going to be the statistic. We were in love and foolish enough to believe that was enough to make a marriage work. We were wrong.

Miami was our new home, though we were rarely there. Craig was in medical school. I was in graduate school and working a full-time and part-time jobs. Even in our pre-elemental life, we didn't have time together. Nor did we know that being married during medical school would significantly increase our odds of getting divorced even more.

It was about to get worse. Residency. We moved to Hawaii, the laid-back, hang loose state. Except we didn't have time for any of that with each other. Residency was far more stressful and time-consuming than medical school. This was before they capped how many hours a resident could work in a row so, Craig routinely worked thirty-six hour stretches at the hospital. I worked full-time running a domestic violence program on the island, but my hours were nights and weekends. When Craig's brother Ryan moved in with us, we had someone to buffer the loneliness we were both feeling. We had a built-in, live-in brother. Someone to come home to, talk with, take on treacherous hikes with, surf or just hang and watch VHI Behind the Music with. We all got along great, although the three of us spending time together was a rarity. With our schedules, we were both spending far more time with Ryan than each other. But, we always had someone to fill the plus one spot at any social function, that inevitably we couldn't fill for each other.

Our contrasting schedules spanned three years. Often the only time we shared was while we slept for a few overlapping hours in the same bed, making getting pregnant a challenge. We tried for several years, which sounds like much more fun than it was. Since Craig was always at work, I'd meet him at a predesignated time at the hospital and then wait an hour for a cut and dried mandatory quickie in the locked resident on-call room. Which was neither sexy nor very hygienic. Despite years of trying to get pregnant in strange places at inconvenient times, somehow, it just didn't happen naturally. Ryan was the one who went with me when I bought the pregnancy tests to confirm that fact.

After Ryan moved back to the mainland, the Army sent us to Oklahoma, Craig's prize for being a stellar resident with an impeccable bedside manner. Soon after, my mom got sick and I went home to take care of her. She passed away two months later. Craig's dad had passed two years earlier. The loss of our parents put an urgency on our determination to start a family. We decided to adopt. The decision was an easy one, the process wasn't. There were criminal background checks to be done. And criminal back ground checks to be mysteriously lost by Russian adoption officials trying to extract money to find them. Russian adoptions, at that time were plagued with corruption. We went packing with a suitcase full of gifts for everyone who had any kind of minor role in the process. The orphanage workers, the driver, the guy who stamped the documents. So about half of Russia. The big bottle of Johnny Walker Black was for the judge, it was her favorite, and we gave it to her in exchange for a son, River.

The week before September 11th, the tragedy that would change everything, we moved to Germany. Our adoption agency sent us photos of siblings and after a butt load of paperwork, made even more complicated by living in Europe, we flew to Russia with River to meet them. But, when we arrived, our agency's Russian counterpart informed us they were no longer available. Matter of factly she said, "You will choose new children now." When you're told something like that in a very stern Russian accent by someone who holds all your really expensive paperwork that took months, your life savings, 4 sets of fingerprints and your potential future children are at stake, you do whatever the hell they say.

Supervised by that passive aggressive Russian lady, we choose Sky and Jade. Then we had to leave them at the orphanage, return home to Germany until a court date to finalize their adoptions was set. The wait was grueling. When it was over and we brought them home to meet their brother, River, he instantly despised his older brother and younger sister. Three months into our family bonding process, Craig got deployed to Iraq. I stayed in Germany alone with 3 kids ages 1, 2 and 3. And started to feel a bit more than passive aggressive myself for doing it on my own.

A year an a half, countless poopy diapers, temper tantrums, time-outs, mommy meltdowns and mistakes later, Craig came home. His debt to the army paid, he was finally a free agent. Then we moved to Colorado on a whim and adopted Ember, who was definitely not a whim. We'd waited years for an opportunity for another child. Now we had four children, the equivalent of two mortgages, a real one and paying monthly installments to buy into a group medical practice, then, we moved to Morocco. Which, as you know was completely stress-free. And that's just the short list.

Twenty years and six months had passed since we committed to living happily ever after, which we completely fucked up and now here we were post-Moroccan rehab. We needed some kind of half way house retreat free of the temptations and stress of the real world to continue to live the clean and sober life. Even if it was just for 10 days, to help us stay on the straight and narrow.

In Costa Rica, where we were going on our big exotic anniversary trip. The forecast was hot and steamy, so I packed light. A string bikini, a halter top or two, a pair of shorts, a sexy skirt and some thongs. When I gave Craig a catwalk preview modeling my bikini.

"Oh my god, you look like a fitness model!" he said.

I'd been a size 2 most of my life, but pole dance packed a whole 5 pounds of muscle onto my formerly petite frame. Standing in front of my new stripper pole in our bedroom studying myself in the full-length mirror, he was right. I had shapely shoulders, capable arms, athletic thighs, a firm round ass and an enviable six pack. I didn't see myself as a scrawny, out of focus wannabe Jennifer Love Hewitt anymore. I could kick her ass, even with her lower center of gravity advantage. I was the same person I'd always been, only better from the inside all the way out.

Unfortunately, it wasn't going to be that kind of no-need-for-a-swimsuit-get-your-freak-on kind of anniversary getaway. Because we were taking the elements on our hot-but-not-in-a-sexy-way-hot celebratory 20 years of marriage vacation. A vacation with kids isn't a vacation at all, it's a trip. It's not that we didn't want to go alone. We totally did. It's just that we couldn't in good conscience ditch them over Christmas. What kind of shitty parents would we be if we did that? Would the elements be scarred forever if we did? What would the neighbors think? Would someone call CPS on us? Why the hell didn't we just dump them on grandma?

Mom guilt, that's why. While I was getting better at recognizing and attempting to deflect the guilt I'd indulged in for far too long, mom guilt was a separate beast. There's no therapy, drug or drink strong enough to alleviate it or the stupid decisions you make while under the influence of it. That's why we begrudgingly took our kids on our twentieth anniversary guilt trip.

It started in the rain forest on a rustic farm far from civilization and any store that sold mosquito repellent, which I forgot to pack. The barebones farmhouse where we stayed had no windows, only screens. Offering no protection from the relentless rainforest mosquitos and only a marginal barrier from the incessant rain and inevitable mud.

Only tourists drove vehicles through the muddy, rough terrain. The natives rode horses and wielded machetes to tame the lush vegetation and defend themselves from the unscrupulous mountain lions and venomous jungle snakes. There were awe inspiring waterfalls, plentiful local organic sustainable foods and horse shit. Massive piles of horse shit, often indistinguishable from the mud after a pelting rain. That was how we liked it—real, gritty, dirty, welty, smelly, swimming in giardia-infested waters pooled at the bottom of waterfalls we'd hiked in to get to with a machete in hand. I added "machete" to my mental wish list. This is how life should be. Muddy and meaningful. Simple and sustainable. Hard and easy at the same time. They needed a town doctor. The elements were thinking the same thing. We could live here, happily. That was the delusion anyway.

~

Craig and I shared the driving through the signless countryside navigating the ceiling fan sized potholes that threatened to strand us on the way to the beach. Without a map. From the backseat the elements gave us a Wrestle Mania play by play of exactly who elbowed whom first. When it was time for lunch, we stopped at a little cafe in a tiny nondescript Costa Rican town in the mountains. Tired, stiff, exhausted and starving. The TV behind the bar played a cheesy David Copperfieldesque magic show in Spanish. Complete with scantily clad assistants in glittery costumes with poorly choreographed 1980's dance moves. It didn't matter what was on; the elements sat comatose watching it eating their sixth day in a row of rice and beans.

That was the only meal of the trip Craig and I ate alone. Except we weren't even alone. I was transfixed watching the only other couple across the room. They didn't seem to notice, they only had eyes for each other, unfazed by their surroundings. I imagined they'd lived in that little town their whole lives. That they'd met when they were young. That he couldn't take his eyes off of her then, the way he can't now. The love between them silently echoed through the room. They didn't need to say a word.

The husband slowly spoon-fed his wheelchair bound wife who was unable to feed herself. His withered frame was still able to push her up the steep hill that ran through the center of town to get her there. But, probably, not for much longer. At their advanced age, they didn't take time or the moments left in them for granted. The way the rest of us who absentmindedly loose track of it do, distracting ourselves with day to day trivialities.

His only focus was her. After all these years, he knew everything about her, all her faults and loved her despite, or maybe even because, of her imperfections. She didn't push him away because she was scared of intimacy. Or maybe she did and he stayed anyway. Knowing she was the one for him. And that running away wouldn't solve their problems. It would just create a whole new array of different ones. So they stayed together for all the trials and tribulations that came their way. Both of them coming to realize that creating a meaningful enduring love took bravery. The children they raised together have long since gone, having kids and challenges of their own. Now here they sit, quietly alone. Together. Silent, because she'd lost the ability to speak. I hope she told him everything he was to her while she still had the chance, that he's everything she's always wanted. He was her life companion, best friend and her rock all along.

## THE AMERICAN OBSESSION

Americans are obsessed with one thing. It's as if we've taken Maslow's Hierarchy of Needs and placed it right on top. The pinnacle of life. Above self-actualization sits happiness. We Americans strive for it but, kinda like sustainable capitalism, it's a myth. Unless I've been misinformed and some entrepreneur has already canned sustainable capitalism for export. Which is of course ridiculous because the only thing America exports anymore is the crazy notion that anyone, even if you're completely devoid of talent and integrity, can be a celebrity. And once you're a celebrity you'll finally be happy.

Years ago when my kids were little, I had this mom friend. More of an acquaintance, really. Her kids were both in elementary school and any time they had a problem, they went to her to solve it. Frequently she asked, "Are you happy?" Not in a condescending way but in a hopeful way so they knew the answer she wanted was yes. I'd never ever in my whole life asked any of my kids if they were happy. I'd never even asked myself that question until I met her, which is why I found it so odd.

When I thought about it, I realized I don't want to know if my kids are happy. They probably aren't. After all, I rarely give them candy, I restrict video games and going to the dollar theatre where we can see a movie everyone else has already seen months ago and given the ending away is an annual event, at best. Even then, I sneak in food from home and embarrass my kids further when we get caught. I think, *At this point in my kids' lives, if they tell me they're happy, I'm a complete failure as a mom.* 'Cause it's not my job to ensure their happiness. It's my job to give them the tools to succeed in life by solving their own problems. Which may or may not result in happiness.

On any given day, I cycle through about twenty-five different emotions. Very rarely is happy one of them. That's not to mean the majority of my feelings are negative. I can be disappointed, frustrated, depressed and enraged. But, I can also be content, proud, pleased and inspired all within fifteen minutes. However, feeling happy is more elusive and more fleeting.

Why does our culture chase happiness like it's a perpetual orgasm? I can tell you with complete certainty it's not attainable. Definitely not sustainable. In America, I feel like an outsider. I'm supposed to follow my bliss, have a nice day or say I'm great even if I feel like stepping off a ledge. Also, do not tell me to smile. I got that one all the time as a sullen-looking little girl. And I will not fake a smile to make you comfortable. Anymore.

Don't get me wrong, I'm not miserable. Anymore. Because I've worked exceptionally hard to get to a place where I feel good about myself. So I can defeat the bad guy...me and her apprentice, lack of confidence. After much introspection and many walks of shame to the self-help section, I'm closer than I've ever been to being content. I can meet happy halfway when it flitters by now and again. But, I'll still feel all the other emotions that come with being human. Let's face it, the relentless pursuit of happiness is destined to become unhappily ever after. I'll take reality with the whole rainbow of fruit flavors...even the bitter ones.

# EPILOGUE

It was only after I finished writing this book that I realized it, the obvious that had eluded me all along. How could I not have known this from the very beginning? I was the kasbah. Me. I'm the fucking kasbah! I had walled myself up like a fortress trying to protect myself from harm. Instead, the distance I put between me and those I loved most isolated me, held me back and sabotaged my marriage, my relationship with the elements and my close friends. I held myself prisoner in my own head. Succumbing to all of my fears and insecurities.

It took being pushed beyond the limits of comfort to confront my inner demons. An inner revolution to tear down the walls I'd hidden behind for so long. Then building myself back up reinforcing the infrastructure, to allow the person I always was to emerge. Just a tad braver and a hell of a lot bolder than I used to be. Only then could I start rebuilding my marriage and being an example for the elements.

Marriage can be the quintessence of nirvana and it can be an unfathomable abyss where one can lose themselves completely. Often it's both and every shade and nuance in between. While it's prodigious, it's also fragile. It takes a very unsexy commitment and the brutally hard work of two merely mortal and fallible people every day. And somehow, despite all my misgivings and mistakes, being ridiculously young and without a backbone to speak of, I undoubtably made the right choice of a man worth going through hell and back for.

I can't say Craig and I will stay together forever and never get divorced. No one can. Either one of us could give it up and bail any day. Especially if we both decide to do it on the same day. But, I don't think we will. Maybe even one day we'll go back to that little village in Costa Rica to retire and you'll find Craig, the town doctor, pushing my wheelchair up the hill to spoon-feed me rice and beans. Unless I'm the one pushing his wheelchair. In Thailand somewhere.

The story isn't over yet. In some ways, it's just the beginning.

# Book Club Discussion Questions

1. What is the significance of the author loving roller derby, something she wasn't good at?

2. How do you know when a relationship is worth keeping? And when is it time to give up?

3. Do you think women can have it all? What does the phrase "have it all" mean to you?

4. What is the biggest risk you've ever taken? Did it pay off?

5. If you could travel anywhere, where would you go? What's stopping you?

6. If you moved to another country with a different cuisine what food from home would you miss the most?

7. What is the weirdest thing you've ever eaten?

8. How does the way in which they travel reflect the Loerzel's as a family?

9. In your opinion, what is the biggest anomaly surrounding the American lifestyle?

10. What do you think is the biggest misconception about Americans?

11. Does labeling and/or diagnosing help or hinder us as a society? And personally?

12. The Quran urges both men and women to dress modestly. It neither mandates nor mentions burkas. Why do you think some women choose wear them?

13. The book says, "Everyone is fucking crazy in some way". What's your crazy? Have you accepted it or changed it?

14. What has been the largest impact of the internet on your life?

15. Has a political agenda ever significantly altered your life path? How?

16. What does it mean to be a feminist? And are you one? Why or why not?

17. What small changes could you make to increase your happiness right now?

18. Your flaws make you human, unique and lovable. Discuss.

# ABOUT THE AUTHOR

Marie is a recovering codependent, perfectionist who's currently fighting the urge to re-edit, tweak and improve this, her debut memoir. She lives in Colorado Springs with her husband and the elements in their home that's slowly sinking into the unstable soil. After returning from Morocco, she fulfilled her promise to the elements to get a dog. They ended up with two rescue dogs, Bonnie and Clyde, who true to their names, are escape artists and bank robbers. Proving, she should never name people or animals ever again. She continues to write, dance and dream about traveling to exotic pungent places. While she loves Colorado, she could be easily tempted to pack the family luggage for anywhere in the world in 5 minutes flat. And maybe she will.

You can find her blog: rockthekasbahafrica.blogspot.com
Follow on Twitter: Rock the Kasbah@Marie Loerzel
Like the Facebook page: Rock the Kasbah